THE PITFALLS OF PIETY FOR MARRIED WOMEN

TWO PRECIOUS SCROLLS OF THE MING DYNASTY

OR,

THE TERRIBLE TRIALS INFLICTED ON DEVOUT MOTHERS BY MEN AND GODS

With detailed descriptions of the abuse suffered
by their children at the hands of second wives

THAT IS,

THE PRECIOUS SCROLL OF THE RED GAUZE

AND

THE PRECIOUS SCROLL OF THE HANDKERCHIEF

Translated from the Chinese on the basis
of the earliest available texts

ALSO INCLUDED AS AN APPENDIX:
Early materials on *The Precious Scroll of Woman Huang*

INTRODUCTION, TRANSLATIONS, AND ANNOTATIONS BY WILT L. IDEMA

CORNELL EAST ASIA SERIES
AN IMPRINT OF
CORNELL UNIVERSITY PRESS
ITHACA AND LONDON

Number 208 in the Cornell East Asia Series

Copyright © 2021 by Cornell University

All rights reserved. Except for brief quotations in a review, this book, or parts thereof, must not be reproduced in any form without permission in writing from the publisher. For information, address Cornell University Press, Sage House, 512 East State Street, Ithaca, New York 14850. Visit our website at cornellpress.cornell.edu.

First published 2021 by Cornell University Press

Librarians: A CIP catalog record for this book is available from the Library of Congress.

ISBN 9781501758362 (hardcover)
ISBN 9781501758386 (pdf)
ISBN 9781501758379 (epub)

Contents

Acknowledgments vii

Chinese Dynasties ix

Introduction   1

   Buddhist Preaching and Storytelling:
     Transformation Texts and Precious
     Scrolls 2
   Female Piety in Precious Scrolls:
     Miaoshan and Woman Huang 6
   Precious Scrolls of the Sixteenth Century:
     Hagiographies, Sectarian Writings, Formal
     Features, and Performance 10
   The *Precious Scroll of the Handkerchief* 14
   The *Precious Scroll of the Red Gauze* 16
   The Third Lad and the Printing History
     of the *Precious Scroll of the Red Gauze* 20

The *Precious Scroll, as Preached by the
Buddha, of Little Huaxian: How Woman
Yang as a Ghost Embroidered Red Gauze*   30

The *Precious Scroll, as Preached by the
Buddha, of the Handkerchief:
How Wang Zhongqing Lost Everything*   100

Appendix: Early Materials on the Legend of Woman Huang   191

After Three Lives of Self-Cultivation Woman Wang Ascends to Heaven in Broad Daylight   191

The *Precious Scroll of Woman Huang* as Partially Included in *The Plum in the Golden Vase*   195

Bibliography   207

Acknowledgments

First of all I have to thank the many Chinese scholars who during the past four decades have worked tirelessly in order to collect, study, and publish precious scrolls, and in that way have made great contributions to the preservation of this genre of popular literature and a better understanding of its many qualities. In preparing the translations in this volume I have especially relied on the critical editions of these texts prepared by Professor Shang Lixin.

Second, I would like to thank Professor Philip Clart for inviting me to participate in the international workshop "Temple, Marketplace, Teahouse and Schoolroom: Local Settings and Social Contexts of Prosimetric Texts in Chinese Popular Traditions" at Leipzig University (July 13, 2019). This stimulated me to formulate some of my thoughts on the development of the *Precious Scroll of the Red Gauze*. I also want to thank Professor Michael Szonyi for his invitation to speak at Harvard University's Fairbank Center for Chinese Studies on September 9, 2019, which allowed me to present the same paper to a quite different audience. The reactions of colleagues and students at both venues have stimulated me to rethink some of my arguments and so, I hope, have contributed to the clarity of the introduction to this volume. I am especially grateful to Dr. Rostislav Berezkin for alerting me in his comments on my paper at the Leipzig workshop to the existence of Ji Qiuyue's recently completed master's thesis on the *Precious Scroll of the Red Gauze* and for his assistance in getting access to her work.

Last but not least I want to express my thanks to the two anonymous readers of the manuscript of this volume. Their detailed comments have been very useful to me in my revision. All remaining mistakes are of course my own.

Chinese Dynasties

Xia	20th–15th century BCE
Shang	15th century–1045 BCE
Zhou	1045 BCE–256 BCE
Qin	221–207 BCE
Han	206 BCE–220 CE
Three Kingdoms	220–280
Wei	220–265
Wu	220–280
Shu-Han	221–265
Jin	265–420
Northern and Southern dynasties	386–589
Sui	581–618
Tang	618–907
Five Dynasties	907–960
Song	960–1279
Northern Song	960–1116
Southern Song	1116–1279
Liao	907–1125
Jin	1115–1234
Yuan	1260–1368
Ming	1368–1644
Qing	1644–1911

THE PITFALLS OF PIETY FOR MARRIED WOMEN

Introduction

Piety in women may be a virtue, but taken to extremes may easily lead to tensions between children and parents, and between husbands and wives, with terrible consequences for all parties concerned. Even when piety attracts the attention of the gods, the immediate result may be negative rather than positive for the families concerned. This volume offers translations of two rare narrative precious scrolls (*baojuan* 寶卷) of the Ming dynasty (1368–1644), the *Precious Scroll of the Red Gauze* (Hongluo baojuan 紅羅寶卷) and the *Precious Scroll of the Handkerchief* (Shoujin baojuan 手巾寶卷), which portray how a wife and mother's piety results in the disruption of her family and terrible misery for her children and her husband; it is only after many years of suffering that these families are reunited and collectively ascend to heaven. If these precious scrolls were written in praise of piety, they equally disclose the many pitfalls of this virtue. In telling their tales, these precious scrolls draw on a wide variety of popular motifs; with their coincidences, miracles, and divine interventions in daily life these texts at times read like gruesome fairy tales. As examples of a highly developed genre of prosimetric storytelling of the Ming, they should appeal to all students of Chinese literature and folklore, and as accounts of female piety in the context of family life they should be informative for students of premodern Chinese religion.

Buddhist Preaching and Storytelling: Transformation Texts and Precious Scrolls

Buddhism has always been a proselytizing religion. Those who have cut off all attachments and left the household and its attendant obligations and affections in order to free themselves from the unending cycle of death and rebirth still need support from donors to survive during their remaining years on earth. The story of the first donation of a monastery and the lavish gifts to the Buddha and his disciples has continued to be one the most popular legends throughout the later history of Buddhism.[1] *Jataka* (tales on the earlier lives of the Buddha Śākyamuni) relate that in his prior incarnations the Buddha was willing to give away not only his own wife and children but even his own body to those in need. Because of their reliance on the gifts of food and other goods from pious donors, monks and nuns never tired of spreading the four noble truths among the surrounding lay populations, teaching the virtue of lay piety not only by the recitation of sutras but also by singing songs and ballads and by telling stories in a fetching manner. According to the first Chinese collection of biographical sketches of eminent monks, when a good preacher speaks about

> death, he makes the heart and body shiver for fear; if he speaks about hell, tears of anxiety gush forth in streams. If he points out earlier karma, it is as if one clearly sees one's deeds from the past; if he predicts the future consequences, he manifests the coming retribution. If he talks about the joys [of the Pure Land], his audience feels happy and elated; if he discourses on the sufferings [of hell], eyes are filled with tears. At that moment the whole congregation is converted and the whole room overcome with emotion; people throw themselves down on the floor, bang their heads against the ground, and beg for grace; each and every one snaps his fingers; everybody recites the name of the Buddha.[2]

Eminent monks drew huge crowds and managed to appeal to all layers of society, adapting subject and manner of presentation to the composition of their audiences; doing so, they engendered strong if not violent emotions.

Buddhism first entered China in the first century AD and established itself as a common aspect of Chinese culture and society by the fourth century at the latest. By the eighth century, Buddhist monks and nuns developed a considerable variety of genres, now collectively known as "transformation texts"

---

1. Mair 1983, 31–86, "Sariputra."
2. Huijiao 1992, 512–13.

(*bianwen* 變文), for preaching to lay audiences.[3] These genres ranged from formalized sutra explanations to expositions on the life of the Buddha, and also extended to long and short stories on pious monks and devout laywomen. Many of these genres used a prosimetric format, that is, they were written in a constant alternation of prose and verse. These texts likely drew on the rich mural paintings that ornamented monasteries and nunneries for illustration, and some may have been accompanied by depictions of episodes as shown on illustrated scrolls.[4] One of the most popular themes in Buddhist bianwen was the story of Maudgalyayana (Mulian 目連) saving his mother from hell.

In the earliest Buddhist tradition Maudgalyayana stands out for his exceptional magical powers. In the Chinese tradition Mulian maintains his magical powers but is better known for his filial piety toward his parents. When Mulian, following the death of his father and mother, has become a monk, he finds out that his father is staying in heaven but that his mother has been relegated to the "prisons in the earth" (*diyu* 地獄) where the souls of the dead are judged. Passing through the courts of the underworld that meticulously keep track of each person's virtues and vices, good deeds and sins, the souls of the dead are either assigned to interminably long periods of gruesome torture in one of the hells or allowed to be reborn. Their manner of rebirth is determined by the amounts of good and evil karma they have accumulated during their lifetime by their deeds, words, and thoughts. Only rarely will human beings be allowed to be reborn immediately in human shape (whether as man or woman); more commonly they will be reborn on one of the other five paths of rebirth, for instance as an animal or a hungry ghost. When Mulian searches the earth prisons for the soul of his mother, he eventually locates her in the Avici hell, the deepest layer of hells. With assistance of the Buddha and the combined power of the Sangha (the community of monks) Mulian eventually is able to deliver his mother from hell, even if initially only in the shape of a dog and a hungry ghost, but eventually she is allowed to join her husband in heaven.[5] The sins that are mentioned as causing her banishment to the Avici hell upon death are listed as the refusal to feed monks with vegetarian food and her own indulgence in meat, but implied in the manner of her punishment is the sexual nature of her crime—women pollute the gods by the blood they shed in menstruation and childbirth and are sinful by the nature

---

3. The meaning of the term *bianwen* has been much discussed. Most scholars now understand "transformation" to meaning a manifestation of a Buddha or deity, so a miracle.

4. Mair 1989. On the use of pictorial aids in the performance of transformation texts, see Mair 1988. The earliest general anthology of bianwen texts in English translation was Waley 1960.

5. Mair 1983, 87–122, "Maudgalyayana, Transformation Text on Mahamaudgalyayana Rescuing His Mother from the Underworld. With Pictures, One Scroll, with Preface."

of their body unless they are able to "slay the red dragon" by a strict abstention from sexual activities and a devout regime of religious exercises, such as sutra reading, reciting the name of the Buddha, practicing seated meditation, maintaining a vegetarian diet (including abstention from alcohol and pungent spices), and making regular donations to monks and nuns.[6]

The texts on Mulian saving his mother from hell probably were intended for performance on the occasion on the Yulanpen Festival on the fifteenth day of the seventh month, the date that was believed to mark the moment his mother was freed from her underworld punishments. This festival is still widely celebrated throughout East Asia. In China it is also known as the Ghost Festival because families make offerings for the posthumous well-being of the deceased.[7] Other bianwen texts too may have been related to major ritual events, but we also have numerous shorter texts known as *yinyuan* 因緣 (tales of causes and condition) that may have been suitable for performance at any occasion when pious donors made a major donation. Many of the tales in this later genre deal with the sufferings and deliverance of laywomen who eventually reach enlightenment, and such tales may have targeted a female audience.

This extensive and varied bianwen literature from the eighth to the tenth century remained unknown for most of the next millennium, because even though book printing was very much a Buddhist invention, bianwen texts were not picked up by the flourishing print industry of the Song dynasty (960–1279), which was primarily geared toward the needs of the students in the state examination system (this became a major means of entrance into the state bureaucracy during these centuries as well as a mechanism to confirm the status of local elites). The rich bianwen literature only became known again following the accidental discovery of a walled-up library cave at Dunhuang around the year 1900. This cave, which had most likely been closed shortly after the year 1000, contained nearly fifty thousand manuscripts as well as a few printed books.[8] The rich and often unique contents of this cave were quickly scattered all over the world, with major holdings now in London, Paris, St. Petersburg, and Beijing, and it took scholars many years to fully realize the special nature of the bianwen texts included among these manuscripts.

Even though we have one or two prohibitions of bianwen performances from the Song, this did of course not mean that monks and nuns stopped

---

6. Cole 1998.
7. Teiser 1988.
8. The earliest dated printed book that has been preserved is a copy of the Diamond Sutra (Jingang jing 金剛經). See Wood and Barnard 2010. For a study and translation of the Diamond Sutra, see Mu Soeng 2000.

preaching. But we have to wait until the thirteenth and fourteenth centuries before we once again encounter vernacular prosimetric texts composed with a lay audience in mind. By this time such texts were no longer designated as bianwen, but came to be known as "precious scrolls." The earliest text that is occasionally called a precious scroll is the *Xiaoshi Jingang keyi* 銷釋金剛科儀 (Ritual amplification explaining the Diamond Sutra; also known as the *Jingang jing keyi* 金剛經科儀 [Diamond Sutra ritual]) of 1242, an edition of the Diamond Sutra with vernacular commentary. The Diamond Sutra, a short Mahayana sutra that had been translated by Kumārajīva (344–409/413), promised unlimited merit to all who read, recite, copy, and multiply its contents. By the Tang dynasty (617–907) it had already established quite a reputation for its capacity to work miracles, creating a veritable cult, especially among lay Buddhists. The many miracles that were credited to the veneration and recitation of the Diamond Sutra were recorded in several collections of wonder tales dedicated to this sutra from the Tang dynasty, and a large selection of such wonder tales is included in the *Taiping guangji* 太平廣記 (Extensive records of the Taiping era), a huge compilation of anomaly tales that was edited in the final years of the tenth century.[9] The Diamond Sutra was widely used in funerary ritual, as it stressed the illusory nature of the body, but many wonder tales also told of devotees who had died but were allowed to return to earth because of their veneration of the sutra. The Diamond Sutra also held that in the mind there is no fundamental difference between male and female, which may explain its attraction for female believers. As a primarily liturgical text, the *Xiaoshi Jingang keyi* remained highly popular throughout the Ming dynasty and the subsequent Qing dynasty (1644–1911), but also remained atypical for the genre of baojuan, to the degree that one may wonder whether it should even be included in the genre.[10]

If one excludes the *Xiaoshi Jingang keyi*, the earliest preserved precious scroll is a text that is once again devoted to the tale of Mulian delivering his mother from her punishments in hell. This long precious scroll most likely was composed in the first half of the fourteenth century and has been partially preserved in a large and beautifully illustrated manuscript dated 1372 that derives from the court of the Northern Yuan dynasty. Yet another also partially preserved illustrated manuscript of this text was produced in 1440 for an imperial concubine of the Ming.[11] The tale of Mulian, in various adaptations, would

---

9. Ho 2019.
10. Overmyer 1999, 34–38.
11. Berezkin 2013c, 109–31.

remain an important topic in precious scroll literature throughout the Ming and Qing dynasties and into modern times.[12]

Female Piety in Precious Scrolls: Miaoshan and Woman Huang

While the tale of Mulian told how mothers could be saved by their sons, some other early narrative precious scrolls taught women how they could save themselves from the cycle of life and death. In his pioneering study of Chinese premodern popular literature, Zheng Zhenduo (1898–1958) in 1938 characterized these works as follows: "They describe how one woman is firmly devoted to the Way, suffers misery and misfortune, but does not swerve from her path despite a hundred frustrations and has the lofty spirit of sacrificing herself for her faith. Their texts may not have been written very well, but this type of theme is rarely encountered in our literature."[13] Probably the most outstanding examples of this subgenre are the *Precious Scroll of Incense Mountain* (Xiangshan baojuan 香山寶卷) and the *Precious Scroll of Woman Huang* (Huangshi baojuan 黃氏寶卷), which both would appear to have been in circulation in their earliest versions at least by the end of the fifteenth century. Both texts are referred to in sources of the first half of the sixteenth century, and both are mentioned in the anonymous vernacular novel *Plum in the Golden Vase* (Jin Ping Mei 金瓶梅), which probably was finished in the 1580s. If the *Precious Scroll of Woman Huang* provided the model for later works in the genre on the pitfalls of piety for married women, the *Precious Scroll of Incense Mountain* focused on the tribulation of a devout girl who refuses to marry, a topic that also would be taken up in many later precious scrolls of the Qing dynasty.[14]

---

12. Berezkin 2017 discusses this text and later adaptations of the legend of Mulian in the precious scroll genre. For a full translation of one of the later precious scroll adaptations of the Mulian legend, the *Precious Scroll of the Three Lives of Mulian* (Mulian sanshi baojuan 目連三世寶卷), see Grant and Idema 2011, 35–145. For a detailed discussion of yet another Qing dynasty adaptation, see Johnson 1995, 55–103.

13. Zheng Zhenduo 1959, 327. Also see Che Xilun (2002, 20–22) for a short characterization of this type of precious scroll.

14. As an example one might mention the *Precious Scroll of Liu Xiang* (Liu Xiang baojuan 劉香寶卷), which tells the story of a pious girl who while still at home convinces her parents to abandon their sinful business of selling meat and wine and to open a vegetarian tea shop. When she is married to the son of a locally prominent family and refuses to consummate her marriage, her mother-in-law first subjects her to all kinds of abuse and then throws her out of the house; the mother also forces her son to marry a second wife. Liu Xiang is reduced to begging but eventually establishes herself as a religious teacher. Her husband, by now a successful bureaucrat, during an illness witnesses the sufferings of his deceased mother and other relatives in hell, and together with his second wife commits himself to the study of Buddhism under Liu Xiang's guidance. Precious scrolls on Liu Xiang were already in

The *Precious Scroll of Incense Mountain* tells of the life of Princess Miaoshan 妙善, the human incarnation of the bodhisattva Guanyin 觀音 (also Guanshiyin 觀世音), who in her female manifestation enjoyed great popular veneration from the eleventh century onward.[15] When Miaoshan's father, King Miaozhuang 妙莊, has no son and orders his three daughters to marry in order to provide him with a grandson, Miaoshan's two elder sisters happily obey, but Miaoshan stubbornly refuses to do so because as a devout girl she wants to become a nun in order to escape from the cycle of life and death. When the arguments of her father, her mother, her sisters, and all officials have failed to change her mind, her father allows her to enter a nunnery, at the same time ordering the abbess to assign her the most onerous duties. When this too fails to change Miaoshan's mind, her father orders her executed, but she is saved at the last moment from the execution ground by divine intervention and taken by a tiger to Incense Mountain, where she devotes herself to religious exercises. When later her father suffers from a debilitating disease, she even offers her own arms and eyes for his recovery. When her father upon his recovery visits her, recognizes her, and is overcome by remorse, she manifests herself in the divine shape of the thousand-armed, thousand-eyed Guanyin and also ensures her family members a divine status. The legend of Miaoshan was first recorded in the very first years of the twelfth century. Later retellings inserted an account of Miaoshan's visit to the underworld, where she saved the souls of sinners.[16] The *Precious Scroll of Incense Mountain* remained extremely popular throughout the Ming and Qing dynasties in several versions, the earliest extant edition of which most likely is an eighteenth-century Vietnamese printing based on a late Ming printing from Nanjing.[17]

In contrast to the tale of Miaoshan, which is set in a mythic past in a mythic country far to the west of China, the setting of the legend of woman Huang is everyday life in China. Woman Huang is portrayed as a woman who from her earliest youth is devoted to Buddhism, and whose preferred religious

---

circulation in the sixteenth century, but the earliest preserved edition dates from the eighteenth century (1774). The *Precious Scroll of Liu Xiang* is discussed, for instance, by Overmyer 1991, 91–120, esp. 109–14; Grant 1995, 29–58; Xu Yunzhen 2016, 198–208; Alexander 2017.

15. Guanyin and Guanshiyin are the Chinese translations of Avalokiteśvara. A detailed account of the development of the Guanyin cult in China is provided in Yü 2001.

16. Dudbridge 1978, 2004. As the legend developed over time, it added a visit to the underworld by Miaoshan following her near-execution and, before the execution scene, an attempt to shame her into submission by parading her as a criminal in front of the whole court. A full translation of the most common version of the *Xiangshan baojuan*, which dates from the nineteenth century, is included in Idema 2008.

17. Overmyer 1999, 38–46; Berezkin and Riftin 2013, 452–55.

exercise consists in the recitation of the *Diamond Sutra*. Despite all the attempts of her parents to turn her attention to more worldly pursuits, she persists in her Buddhist piety, and her parents eventually marry her off to the butcher Zhao Lingfang 趙令方. When she has been married to this man for twelve years and has given him three children, she proposes to him that he should abandon his sinful life as a butcher and join her in her Buddhist devotions. When he rejects this request (because he is making good money, because no one has ever returned from hell to prove its existence, and because women are inherently far more sinful than men), she requests permission to sleep alone, to which request her husband agrees after she has shown her complete mastery of the *Diamond Sutra*. But this perfect recitation of the sutra also attracts the attention of King Yama, the ruler of the underworld, who has her summoned before him. Taking her leave of her husband and children, woman Huang follows the emissaries of King Yama to the underworld, where she is treated to a display of all the tortures sinners have to endure. When she has answered all of King Yama's questions on the *Diamond Sutra* to his full satisfaction, she is allowed to be reborn on earth, this time as a man; however, her original identity is inscribed on one of her sides. Born into a rich family, the young man quickly passes the imperial examinations. Appointed as magistrate to his original home town, he summons the original husband, Zhao Lingfang, to whom he discloses his original identity as woman Huang, whereupon husband, wife, and children all ascend to heaven. Some versions add a third life at the beginning of the legend that describe woman Huang as the reincarnation of a pious donor of the Buddhist community.[18]

The legend of woman Huang (or woman Wang 王氏, as some Chinese dialects do not distinguish *huang* and *wang*) circulated widely not only as a precious scroll in late imperial times but also in various other genres of prosimetric literature,[19] and the legend was also brought to the stage by the last century of the Ming.[20] The earliest version preserved as a precious scroll is represented by the substantial excerpts from the text in chapter 74

---

18. Grant 1989; Shang Lixin and Che Xilun 2015, 278–324.

19. For a full translation of a version in verse published in the early decades of the twentieth century in Shanghai, see Grant and Idema 2011, 147–229; for a full translation of the version in women's script from Jiangyong, see Idema 2009, 135–57. For a discussion of the enduring popularity of the tale of woman Huang among the Bai ethnicity in Yunnan Province, see Bryson 2015.

20. Dramatic performances of the legend of woman Huang remained popular in the first half of the twentieth century but were prohibited in 1951 in the People's Republic of China. When such plays were briefly revived in 1957, they were quickly condemned once again. The story of woman Huang was also included in some of the dramatic adaptations of the story of Mulian.

of *Plum in the Golden Vase*. A full translation of this version, which highlights the formal features of this text, is included in the appendix to this volume,[21] together with a prose summary of the legend included as the last miracle tale in the *Jingangjing zhengguo* 金剛經証果 (Proofs and fruits of the Diamond Sutra) and titled *After Three Lives of Self-Cultivation Woman Wang Ascends to Heaven in Broad Daylight* (Sanshi xiuxing Wangshinü bairi shengtian 三世修行王氏女白日升天). The *Jingangjing zhengguo* is credited to a monk of the Song dynasty but known only from a 1592 edition. In this version woman Huang as a young girl is abused by her stepmother, whose own son attempts to murder the girl's father but ends up killing his own mother, whereupon he accuses woman Huang of the murder. Condemned to death by strangulation, she is rescued by divine intervention, whereupon her stepbrother accuses her once more of murdering his mother, but this time he is condemned to death by slow slicing. Frustrated by her incessant recitation of the *Diamond Sutra*, her father then marries her off to butcher Zhao.[22] On one hand, this account reads very much as a summary of a precious scroll, and its position in the *Jingangjing zhengguo* strengthens one's suspicion that this might be a later addition to the text, reflecting the popularity of the *Precious Scroll of Woman Huang* during the sixteenth century.[23] On the other hand, an account of woman Huang's devotion to the *Diamond Sutra* may already have been translated into the Jürched language and printed during the Jin dynasty (1115–1234) in 1183,[24] and a story about a woman Wang who is resurrected from death because of her devotion to the *Diamond Sutra* is already known from the Tang (617–906),[25] all suggesting that the legend of woman Huang and her devotion to the *Diamond Sutra* may have known a long development during the many centuries from the Tang till the Ming.

---

21. For an alternative translation, including the description of the performance and the introductory sermon, see Roy 2010, 437–52. Li Shiyu 李世瑜 (1922–2010) claimed in Li Shiyu 1961, 8 (entry 071) that these extracts derived from a Ming-dynasty printed version of the legend of woman Huang titled *Foshuo Huangshinü kanjing baojuan* 佛說黃氏女看經寶卷 (The precious scroll as preached by the Buddha on the daughter of the Huang family reading the sutra) in his collection, but that version, if it still exists, is inaccessible (Shang Lixin and Che Xilun 2015, 317). Li Shiyu's personal collection of precious scrolls was confiscated during the Cultural Revolution and never returned to him. It should be noted that Li Shiyu 1961, 40, entry 336, lists the source of the excerpts in the novel as unidentified.

22. Shang Lixin and Che Xilun 2015, 279–80.

23. Shang Lixin and Che Xilun 2015, 280.

24. Liu Lili 2012, 35; Shang Lixin and Che Xilun 2015, 280. The Chinese title of the translated text is listed as *Huangshinü shu* 黃氏女書 (The book on the daughter of the Huang family).

25. Li Fang 1960, 618, "Wangshi 王氏." This story was earlier included in Duan Chengshi 段成式 (800–863), *Jingang jing jiuyi* 金剛經鳩異 (Collected miracles of the Diamond Sutra), a ninth-century collection of tales of wonder devoted to the Diamond Sutra. For a full translation of this tale as included in *Jingang jing jiuyi*, see Ho 2019, 401.

Precious Scrolls of the Sixteenth Century: Hagiographies, Sectarian Writings, Formal Features, and Performance

As the *Precious Scroll of the Handkerchief* and the *Precious Scroll of the Red Gauze* in their earliest preserved versions most likely date from the last century of the Ming dynasty, they also show the impact of new developments in the genre over the course of the sixteenth century. This period is best known in the history of Chinese religion for the emergence of numerous new religions (or sects). These sects often adopted the format of precious scrolls to propagate their teachings. At the same time, local cults adopted the format for hagiographies of their deities. Both kinds of precious scrolls adopted the same highly specific format for the composition of their texts.

Woman Huang was, unlike Guanyin, not venerated as a deity in her own right, but several other early narrative precious scrolls retell as a hagiography the mortal life of deities and, upon their death, the miracles they performed for the sake of their believers. Some of these deities have, like Guanyin, a clear Buddhist character, but others represent local cults. A good example of a relatively early precious scroll devoted to a local deity is the *Precious Scroll of the Immortal Maiden Equal to Heaven* (Pingtian xiangu baojuan 平天仙姑寶卷), which is devoted to a female deity who was venerated in Western Gansu; this deity not only defended the Chinese borders against foreign invaders but also punished those men and women who offended against family morals. Her precious scroll most likely dates from the sixteenth century but has been preserved in an edition of 1698 that was sponsored by the military governor of Gansu and had been edited and expanded by an official waiting for appointment.[26] Hagiographies of local deities continue to be part of the repertoire of precious scrolls in places where they are still currently performed.[27]

Not only local cults but also the new religions of the Ming dynasty and beyond made use of precious scrolls. Starting from the fifteenth century, the Ming dynasty witnessed the rise of many new religions or sects that proclaimed

---

26. For a full translation of this text, see Idema 2015, 23–262.

27. Another example of an early hagiographic precious scroll, this time from the Jiangnan region, is provided by the *Mengjiang baojuan* 猛將寶卷 (also known as *Tiancao baojuan* 天曹寶卷), dedicated to Fierce General Liu 劉猛將軍, who protects crops against locusts. The earliest preserved manuscript dates from 1663 (Che Xilun 1998, 23), so the text most likely was composed in the late Ming. Berezkin (2013a, 73–111) discusses a number of precious scrolls dedicated to local deities. He treats these texts as products of the latest phase in the development of precious scrolls. While this may apply to the particular texts discussed in his article, it does not apply to hagiographic baojuan dedicated to local gods in general. The precious scrolls discussed in Berezkin and Goossaert (2012–2013, 295–326) also date from the second half of the nineteenth century or later.

a new dispensation of the truth. Largely based on the popular Buddhism of the time, many of these new religions also incorporated elements of Confucianism and Daoism. In the teachings of some of these sects the Unborn Old Mother (Wusheng laomu 無生老母, also known as the Venerable Mother and the Eternal Mother) played a major role.[28] The Unborn Old Mother gave birth to humankind in a mythic past. Ever since her children have left her and have been caught up in the cycle of life and death, she has longed for their return and therefore time and again has sent teachers down to earth to reveal the truth, but her sinful offspring too often have not heeded their warnings. Many of these new religions present themselves as a final chance for a limited number of elect to be saved and to be reunited with the Old Mother. Such beliefs in the ultimate deliverance of a select few may be combined with various Buddhist teachings, such as a fervent belief in the power of the Buddha Amitābha to save all who piously recite his name, and/or the equally fervent belief in the imminent arrival of the Buddha Maitreya, who will be the Buddha of the next (eighty-first) kalpa and who will gather his faithful at the Dragon-Flower congregation.[29] The overwhelming majority of preserved precious scrolls of the sixteenth and seventeenth centuries are so-called sectarian precious scrolls, in which the teachers of these new religions expound their teachings.[30]

By the sixteenth century precious scrolls had acquired a very stable but also highly specific format. Many scholars stress the direct descent of precious scrolls from transformation texts, and they see this descent exemplified by the development of the transformation texts on Mulian saving his mother into the precious scrolls on the same topic. The bianwen genre that may have most successfully survived the transition from Tang to Song (and later) would appear to have been the *yinyuan* 因緣 (tales of causes and conditions). That term continued to be used in late imperial China, and the *Xiangshan baojuan* refers even in its nineteenth-century edition to its own text as a yinyuan.[31] But

---

28. "Unborn" means uncreated, and therefore not subject to the cycle of growth and decay, death and rebirth, but eternal and unchanging. Some scholars prefer to translate "wusheng" as "unbegotten." For a systematic discussion of the cult of the Unborn Old Mother, see Shek 1999. Also see Overmyer 1976, 135–41; Seiwert 2003, 246ff.

29. The reunion with the Old Mother, the rebirth in the Western Paradise, and the participation in the Dragon-Flower Assembly during the eighty-first and final kalpa all are metaphorical expressions for deliverance from the cycle of life and death by realizing one's inborn Buddha-nature and one's mystical union with the ultimate void.

30. Overmyer 1999, passim.

31. At times the meaning of the term *yinyuan* seems to have lost its Buddhist connotation and simply means "story," but at other times it still clearly refers to proselytizing Buddhist tales, for instance when in chapter 5 of the sixteenth-century novel *Shuihuzhuan* 水滸傳, Lu Zhishen 魯智深 after leaving the monastery claims, "With abbot Zhen on Wutaishan I learned to tell *yinyuan* so I can fully convert even people of iron or stone" (Shi Nai'an and Luo Guanzhong 2009, vol. 2, 393). For Buddhist tales one also encounters the expression *yinguo* 因果 (cause-and-fruit).

despite this undeniable connection between bianwen and baojuan, one also has to point out the formal differences between the two genres. The transformation texts, including the yinyuan texts, tell their story in a simple alternation of passages in prose and passages in verse; these passages in verse are commonly written in seven-syllable lines. This applies also to Dunhuang versions of the tale of Mulian, one of which is a yinyuan text. The fourteenth-century precious scroll on the legend of Mulian, however, tells its story in a great number of sections each of which consists of an introductory paragraph in prose, a couplet of two seven-syllable lines, a passage in verse (made up of eight seven-syllable lines), a short "hymn" (mostly made up of four-syllable lines),[32] and a quatrain. The text of the Vietnamese edition of the *Precious Scroll of Incense Mountain* follows the same pattern, but in this text the passages in verse have been expanded to sixteen seven-syllable lines, while each section opens with a paragraph from the Heart Sutra (the chapter in the Lotus Sutra dedicated to Guanyin), which will have been recited in the specific manner of sutra recitation.[33] This may well mean that this text originated in the fifteenth century, because in the precious scrolls of the early sixteenth century each section not only acquired a numbered heading but was also introduced by a song or songs to a popular tune, while the passages in verse, increasingly composed in ten-syllable lines, had a different length in each section. The excerpts from the *Precious Scroll of Woman Huang* in *Plum in the Golden Vase* clearly derive from a version that not only included a song at the heading of each section but also had started to make the shift from seven-syllable lines to ten-syllable lines in the verse passages.[34]

The inclusion of songs for several tunes and the use of the ten-syllable line alongside the seven-syllable line in the verse passages may have enhanced the attractive power of the performance, but also put higher demands on the performer (whether male or female), who now had to be not only a clear reader

---

32. The word "hymn" is used in reference to the form, not to the content.
33. For a discussion of the formal aspects of this text, see Berezkin and Riftin 2013, 476–81. It should be stressed that the prose text that follows each paragraph from the sutra in each section makes no attempt to explain the text or the message of the sutra but continues the narrative of the preceding section. This text is therefore quite different in structure from the *Jingang jing keyi* and the few other precious scrolls that quote sutras.
34. The specific format of sixteenth-century precious scrolls clearly distinguishes the genre from other forms of prosimetric literature that have been preserved from the Ming dynasty. Ballad-stories (*cihua* 詞話) are written in an alternation of prose and verse. These verse sections are composed mostly in seven-syllable lines, but one occasionally also encounters verse sections in ten-syllable lines. The narrative *daoqing* 道情 also are made up of an alternation of prose and verse. But in this case the verse passages are overwhelmingly written to a variety of allometric song tunes, with only a few passages in ballad verse. Alternatively, the verse passages are mostly composed in ballad verse, with a sprinkling of songs to allometric tunes. From the Ming we also have long narrative ballads that are composed completely in verse, such as ballad texts (*ciwen* 詞文) and wooden-fish books (*muyushu* 木魚書).

of prose and a fine reciter of various kinds of verse but also an excellent singer of numerous tunes. The most detailed descriptions of performances of precious scrolls that have been preserved from the sixteenth century are those that are provided by *Plum in the Golden Vase*. This novel on several occasions (chapters 38, 39, 51, 73, 74, and 82) describes the performances of precious scrolls in the inner apartments of the household of a wealthy merchant, the debauchee Ximen Qing 西門慶. These performances are sponsored by his pious wife Wu Yueniang 吳月娘, who invites local nuns to perform precious scrolls for the edification and entertainment of herself and female relatives (on occasion male relatives also attend).[35] It would be wrong, however, to conclude from these descriptions that the performers and audiences of precious scrolls will have been primarily female. Monks and nuns will have preached the precious scrolls to male, female, and mixed audiences at their institutions; priests will have preached the hagiographies of local deities to local audiences; and sect leaders will have preached their precious scrolls to their flocks; while the availability of written and printed copies allowed laypeople to perform in front of their families or larger crowds. All such performances were interactive affairs, as the listeners were expected to join in the recitation of the names of the Buddha and/or to echo the last words of each couplet.[36]

The two narrative precious scrolls that form the core of this volume not only display the formal characteristics of the fully developed precious scroll of the sixteenth century but also show the influence of the new religions of the Ming dynasty, especially in their ritual opening and ritual conclusion of the text, while one of them may have originated in a hagiographical text. Both their formal features and their references to the Unborn Old Mother identify the *Precious Scroll of the Handkerchief* and the *Precious Scroll of the Red Gauze* as works of the sixteenth or seventeenth century. Later precious scrolls of the eighteenth century and beyond (including other versions of the two texts translated in this volume) tend to be much simpler in form. They usually abandon the division into chapters, and while they may maintain the couplet between a prose passage and the following section in verse, they often omit the hymn and quatrain that follow the verse section. With the increasing suppression of sectarian religions from the eighteenth century onward,

---

35. These descriptions have been studied repeatedly. See, for instance, Sawada Mizuho 1975, 285–99; Carlitz 1986, 59–66; Che Xilun 1990, 360–74; Johnson 1995; Yang Zihua 2006, 34–39; Dong Zaiqin and Li Yu 2008; Xue Runmei 2018, 17–22.

36. Johnson 1995 collects and analyzes the descriptions of precious scroll performance that were available in written sources up to 1990. Since that time we have numerous descriptions of contemporary performances, both from Western Gansu (Idema 2015, 7–9) and from the Wu dialect area (Bender 2001; Berezkin 2011a, 2011b, 2013b, 2015; Sun 2019).

later narrative precious scrolls also tend to omit references to the Unborn Old Mother.

The *Precious Scroll of the Handkerchief*

The story of the *Precious Scroll of the Handkerchief* starts very much in the manner of the *Precious Scroll of Woman Huang*: the female protagonist Zhang Suzhen 張素真, the pious wife of the rich man Wang Zhongqing 王忠慶 and the mother of their two children (their son Wang Tianlu 王天祿 and their daughter Huixiang 茴香), suggests to her husband that she and her children live by themselves in one side of the house so that she may be able to devote herself fully to her religious exercises—but whereas the dying woman Huang urged her husband never to remarry, Zhang Suzhen unwisely suggests to her husband that he marry a second wife to take care of the household and live with him in the other side of the house. Her husband takes her up on this proposal and soon finds a concubine, woman Li 李氏, in the brothel district. This woman sets her husband up against his first wife by suggesting that Zhang Suzhen's generosity toward monks is sapping the family fortune, and so when Zhang Suzhen persists in feeding monks and making donations to them, her husband gives her a beating and later, when drunk, even rips out one of her eyes, whereupon Zhang Suzhen, abandoning her children, flees the house at night and eventually joins a nunnery.

Once she has rid herself of the lady of the house, woman Li sets out to rid herself of her two stepchildren by abusing them in every way possible whenever Wang Zhongqing is away from home collecting loans. Unable to stand his children's weeping at home, Wang Zhongqing allows himself to be persuaded to join some other rich men on a trading trip to Hangzhou. During his absence from home woman Li eventually sets out to murder the two children, but, warned by the gods, they make their escape in time. Afraid they made be easily recognized and caught if they stay together, they decide to split up, and the elder brother Wang Tianlu gives his younger sister Huixiang a handkerchief as a token to recognize each other if they may meet at some future date. The girl eventually comes to the nunnery where her mother is staying and also becomes a nun. Her brother, when sleeping at night in the Guan Yu 關羽 temple at Tong Pass, is instructed by this martial deity in all military arts and joins the army.[37] After achieving great merits in battles against

---

37. The mortal Guan Yu (d. 2019) was one of the sworn brothers of Liu Bei, the founder of the Shu-Han dynasty in Sichuan. Guan Yu was widely venerated as a deity from the Song dynasty onward

INTRODUCTION   15

the Jūrched, he is promoted to high office and receives the only daughter of his commander as wife.

In the meantime, Wang Zhongqing on his return from Hangzhou barely survives a shipwreck when crossing the Yangzi. Begging his way back home, he finds out that his house has been completely destroyed by fire, so he and woman Li have to survive as beggars. When Wang Tianlu, following a meeting with the emperor, is on his way to his home in order to present sacrifices at the ancestral graves, he is reunited with his mother and sister when visiting their nunnery, as he recognizes the handkerchief his sister is carrying. When he organizes grand celebrations including a food distribution to the poor, Wang Zhongqing and woman Li at every meal get nothing to eat because each time they end up at the end of the line, and when they complain about their treatment at night, they are reunited with the other members of the family. Wang Tianlu orders that a beating be administered to woman Li, but when his father tries to intervene on her behalf, he becomes so enraged that he has her beaten to death. After the celestial background of Wang Zhongqing, Zhang Suzhen, Huixiang, and Wang Tianlu and his wife have been disclosed, these five persons return to heaven.

The *Precious Scroll of the Handkerchief* has been preserved in a considerable number of manuscripts of the nineteenth and twentieth centuries, some of which sport different titles, such as *Precious Scroll of Feeding Monks* (Zhaiseng baojuan 齋僧寶卷) and *Precious Scroll of Urging One's Husband to Take a Concubine* (Quanfu taoqie baojuan 勸夫討妾寶卷).[38] The earliest manuscript of the *Precious Scroll of the Handkerchief* would appear to be the manuscript in the collection of the late Zhou Shaoliang 周紹良 (1917–2005), which was produced during the Ming dynasty.[39] In this manuscript, fully titled the *Precious Scroll, as Preached by the Buddha, of the Handkerchief: How Wang Zhongqing Lost Everything* (Foshuo Wang Zhongqin dashisan Shoujin baojuan 佛說王忠慶大失散手巾寶卷), the text shows all the typical formal characteristics of precious scrolls of the sixteenth and seventeenth centuries. The text is divided into thirty sections, each made up of an opening song, a passage in prose, a couplet of two seven-syllable lines, a passage in ballad verse (with one exception all in ten-syllable lines[40]), a "hymn," and a quatrain. The liturgical opening of the text and its

---

and eventually achieved imperial rank as god of war during the Qing dynasty. For the origin and development of the veneration of the deified Guan Yu, see Haar 2017.

38. Li Yu 2010, 124–26.
39. Zhou Shaoliang 1990.
40. This one exception is a *lianhualao* 蓮花落 (begging song). Such begging songs are frequently incorporated in narrative precious scrolls. In performance they come with their own refrain from the audience. Liu Huiru 2018 limits his discussion to examples from the Qing dynasty and does not discuss

liturgical conclusion are identical to those found in many sectarian texts, and also make reference to the Unborn Old Mother, but there are no references to this cult in the main body of the text. The scholar Che Xilun has suggested that the manuscript represents an adaptation of the story by a preacher belonging to one of the new religions of the Ming,[41] but it is of course also possible that an anonymous editor has borrowed the ritual introduction and conclusion without being too much concerned with their possible sectarian content. The translation in this volume is based on the text of the Ming manuscript as edited by Shang Lixin in her *Baojuan congchao*.[42]

The *Precious Scroll of the Red Gauze*

While woman Huang displays her piety by her assiduous recitation of the Diamond Sutra and Zhang Suzhen by her rich gifts to monks, woman Yang, the female protagonist of the *Precious Scroll of the Red Gauze* (Hongluo baojuan 紅羅寶卷), does so by her embroidery skills. Like woman Huang's recitation skills, her devout embroidery causes her soul to be taken to the underworld before her time, but as care is taken that her corpse will not decompose during her stay in the City of the Unjust Deaths,[43] she is eventually able to return to her own body. The story takes place at some time during the Tang dynasty at an unidentified locality, and starts when the rich man Zhang 張員外 is humiliated by young men at a party because he has no son. He and his wife, woman Yang 楊氏, thereupon visit the local temple of the Third Lad (Sanlang miao 三郎廟), and, making a vow, pray for a child. The Third Lad arranges that a golden lad who had been condemned to be reborn on earth for some minor mistake will be born as the son of the couple. The couple is overjoyed when the child is born, but they forget to fulfill their vow, so when the infant, named Huaxian 化仙, turns three, the Third Lad takes his soul away. The disconsolate mother now promises the god to embroider a precious curtain of red gauze to protect his image.[44] Hua-

---

the begging songs incorporated in *Shoujin baojuan* and *Hongluo baojuan*. Huang Jing (2013, 412–16) discusses examples of *lianhualao* in two contemporary precious scrolls from Jingjiang.

41. Che Xilun 2007, 9–13, and 2009, 528–37.
42. Shang Lixin 2018, 103–38.
43. The City of the Unjust Deaths is a special section of the underworld reserved for the souls of those people who have passed away before their preordained dates of death, for instance because they died of an accident, were murdered, or committed suicide. They have to wait there until the preordained dates of death arrive before they can appear before the underworld judges. Instead of "city" it might be more appropriate to speak of "a walled enclosure."
44. On embroidery as a devotional practice of elite women in late imperial China, see Fong 2004, 19–20, and Li Yuhang 2012. See also Zhang Tianyou and Zhang Xipin 2019.

xian immediately returns to life, but it takes his mother three years to complete this curtain, which shows all the phenomena of heaven and earth.

When the two elder and the two younger brothers of the Third Lad are shown the curtain, they become jealous and decide to fetch the soul of woman Yang and take her to the City of The Unjust Deaths (Wangsicheng 枉死城) in the underworld, so her soul will be able to embroider the same curtains for each of them—when she will have completed her assignment in twelve years, her soul will be released again. Before her death woman Yang (like woman Huang) implores her husband not to remarry, but rich man Zhang is soon persuaded by the wily matchmaker woman Kang 康氏 to marry a woman You 尤氏, who brings a son of her own into the marriage. Huaxian longs for his mother, gets into frequent fights with his elder stepbrother, and stirs up the animosity of his evil stepmother, who uses the frequent absences of the father to abuse the boy. When she has nearly beaten the boy to death and sprinkled his skin with thorns, rich man Zhang administers his new wife a beating, but the next time he leaves she tries to kill the boy by throwing him into a wok of boiling water—the boy is saved in the nick of time by the intervention of the Third Lad. The same deity also intervenes when she tries to poison her stepson.

When rich man Zhang has left home to take up a position as commandant at Jiujiang, he is defeated by a pirate, condemned to death, and locked up in prison in the Capital. Woman You now makes up her mind to kill Huaxian and has a steel knife made for the purpose. But when at midnight she approaches the bed in which Huaxian and his elder stepbrother are sleeping, the Third Lad has changed their places, and in the dark woman You ends up murdering her own son. She takes revenge by accusing Huaxian in court of the crime, and convinces the disbelieving judge by offering him a substantial bribe. Huaxian is condemned to death, but when he is about to be executed, he is lifted from the execution ground by the Third Lad manifesting himself as a whirlwind. When Huaxian has been deposited on the ground again, Huaxian is told to go and find his father.

When little Huaxian after a long trip comes to the capital and meets with his father, he saves him from starvation by begging. After he has taken care of his father by begging for eleven years, a princess chooses a groom by throwing an embroidered ball into a crowd. Because the ball falls into Huaxian's begging bowl, he becomes her husband as prince consort. When the princess notes his sadness, he tells her his story, whereupon she informs her father the emperor, and the latter frees rich man Zhang and gives Huaxian three thousand troops to go and take revenge on his enemies. The moment woman You has been arrested and begs for mercy, woman Yang has finished her embroidery job in the underworld and calls from her coffin to be released. When woman Yang has been reunited with her husband and son (and her daughter-in-law), she begs her son to pardon woman You and her accomplices, and he eventually agrees to her request.[45]

The tale is rather complicated, but it is, like the *Precious Scroll of the Handkerchief*, made up of a hodgepodge of conventional motifs. Many tales start with a description of a childless rich couple praying for a son; when a banished celestial is born to them, he is bound to encounter many torments and tribulations before he will be able to return to heaven. Embroidery (and weaving) skills are often praised at length in other prosimetric texts. Mothers who before their early death beg their husbands to take good care of their child(ren), and therefore not to remarry, are commonly encountered stock characters, as are venal go-betweens and widows who are eager to remarry and prove to be evil stepmothers. If this story stands out, it is not for the evil nature of woman You per se, but for the number of attempts it takes her to get rid of Huaxian. The evil stepmother who while trying to kill her stepchild murders her own son is also encountered in other stories. The idea that money can buy the cooperation of initially well-intentioned men is of course also not original with this tale. The filial piety of Huaxian as displayed in his devotion to his mother and in his support of his father must of course be rewarded, and the sudden reversal of fortune by catching the ball that is thrown into a crowd of suitors by a princess or some other noble young lady seeking a groom is one of the most common ways to do so. And once the young man has married into the imperial family, all problems are solved.[46]

The *Precious Scroll of the Red Gauze*, also known as the *Precious Scroll of the Stepmother* (Wanniang baojuan 晚娘寶卷), was quite popular in the late Qing dynasty and the first half of the twentieth century. In his *Zhongguo baojuan congmu*, Che Xilun lists, in addition to over thirty manuscripts from this period (starting with one from 1829), no less than six different lithographic editions

---

45. This summary is based on the modern edition of the earliest preserved edition in Shang Lixin 2018, 75–102.

46. Ji Qiuyue 2019, 37–41. Sawada Mizuho 1975, 296–97, goes so far as to characterize this precious scroll as "an inept and primitive work." His summary of the contents is based on a manuscript in his possession in which the action of the story has been moved to the reign of Emperor Renzong of the Song, and in which the place of the action has been specified. He also notes that in one of the lithographic editions, the time of the action is specified as the reign of Emperor Xuanzong of the Tang. The temple where husband and wife pray for a son in Sawada's manuscript is the Wusheng shenmiao 五聖神廟 (divine temple of the five sages).

from the 1910s and 1920s.[47] That list, as we know, is far from complete.[48] When after the Cultural Revolution (1966–1978) precious scroll recital was allowed once again from the 1980s onward, the *Precious Scroll of the Red Gauze* turned out to be quite popular in Western Gansu. Most of the recent local collections of precious scrolls from this region include the item.[49] But as far as I know, none of the local collections from the Wu dialect area do so, despite the widespread popularity of the story in that region up to the middle of the twentieth century.[50]

The *Precious Scroll of the Red Gauze* also can claim to be one of the earliest precious scrolls. A performance of this title is already mentioned in chapter 82 of *Plum in the Golden Vase*. The novel does not quote from the text or otherwise give any indication of the contents, which suggests that this was a popular text at the time and that the novelist could assume that his readers would be acquainted with the contents. We do have a copy of a printed edition from the sixteenth century if not earlier. This edition, fully titled the *Precious Scroll, as Preached by the Buddha, of Little Huaxian: How Woman Yang as a Ghost Embroidered Red Gauze* (Foshuo Yangshi guixiu hongluo Huaxiange baojuan 佛說楊氏鬼繡紅羅化仙哥寶卷) and kept in the Shanxi Provincial Museum, has been reproduced by Ma Xisha in his *Zhonghua zhenben baojuan*.[51] The text in this edition is made up of twenty-two numbered sections; the ritual introduction

---

47. Che Xilun 1998, 38, 107–9. The five manuscripts formerly in the collection of Fu Xihua are described in considerable detail in Wu Ruiqing 2018, 127–30. In Fu Xihua's own catalogue of the genre, published in 1951 as Fou Si-houa, "Catalogue de Pao-kiuan 寶卷總錄," he mentions that his own collection also includes a printed edition of the Kangxi period. The collection of the Suzhou Theater Museum includes thirteen manuscript versions and one lithographic edition of the precious scroll. See Guo Lamei 2018, 50–52. The earliest manuscript in this collection dates from 1855. Che Xilun (2009, 518) also mentions a *Jishan qiu'er Hongluo baojuan* 積善求兒紅羅寶卷 (Precious scroll of red gauze: Seeking a son by amassing good deeds) in two parts that is listed in a report on the activities of the Hongyangjiao 紅陽教 in Dezhou in 1817. No copy of this edition has been preserved, but the fact that it consisted of two parts suggests a relatively late date.

48. For an updated list, see Ji Qiuyue 2019, 12–20. The known manuscripts from the period 1800–1949 overwhelmingly originated from the Wu dialect area of Zhejiang and Jiangsu. The lithographic editions were produced in Shanghai and Hangzhou. These Wu dialect area versions represent two closely related but distinct families of the tale (Ji Qiuyue 2019, 20–25, 41–46).

49. Shang Lixin and Che Xilun 2015, 506–11, describe a manuscript of 1832 in the possession of the authors, an undated manuscript in the library of the Institute of Literature of the Chinese Academy of Social Sciences, and the various versions of this precious scroll recorded in recent years in Western Gansu. The majority of the versions published in Western Gansu in recent decades, usually titled *Xiu hongluo baojuan* 繡紅羅寶卷 (Precious scroll of embroidering the red gauze), belong to a quite distinct family of texts. Woman Yang is, for instance, treated to extended tours of the hells, allowing her to witness the punishments of sinners in detail (Ji Qiuyue 2019, 46–48).

50. Ji Qiuyue (2019, 67–81) provides a critical edition of a manuscript of 1897, now in the Shanghai Library, that was produced by one Yin Shouqing 殷綬卿.

51. Ma Xisha 2012, vol. 7, 191–244.

and conclusion are largely identical to those in the *Precious Scroll of the Handkerchief*. The original copy is atypically preserved in a butterfly binding,[52] and as a result many lines are not legible in this reprint. Fortunately, Shang Lixin in her 2015 *Baojuan congchao* has provided a typeset edition, in which the text of the Ming edition as reproduced by Ma Xisha has been collated with two subsequent but still early manuscripts of this text.[53] This is the edition I have used as the basis for my translation.

The Third Lad and the Printing History of the *Precious Scroll of the Red Gauze*

Whereas Zhang Suzhen and her children receive divine support from a host of different deities (the Medicine King, Guan Yu, the god of the soil), a single deity, the enigmatic Third Lad, plays a central role the *Precious Scroll of the Red Gauze*. A quick search of the local gazetteers included in the first and second collection of local gazetteers in the Erudition Database reveals that temples to several deities named the Third Lad are recorded from all over China in gazetteers starting from the sixteenth century but are quite rare before that time. For instance, a temple to an otherwise unidentified Third Lad in Dong Village twenty-seven kilometers outside Yongji that now has disappeared included a stage that was constructed in 1322 and is still standing.[54] This would suggest that a cult to the Third Lad may be traced back to the early fourteenth century if not earlier. The same Third Lad may have had more temples in his honor in southern Shanxi and northern Henan. One modern oral story claims that a temple to the Third Lad in Yangcheng had been established by Liu Xiu 劉秀, the founder of the Eastern Han dynasty (25–220). Once when Liu Xiu's army in the sixth month found its way blocked by a raging Yellow River, Liu Xiu

---

52. A butterfly binding is very rare for precious scrolls. In a butterfly binding the sheet carrying two pages is folded with the printed pages facing each other. These folded pages are then glued together at the fold. If the pages cannot be separated for reproduction (as is easily done in stitch bindings), the lines close to the fold may not show up in the reproduction. Almost all early precious scrolls are produced in sutra bindings (harmonica bindings).

53. Shang Lixin 2018, 75–102, has used the manuscript of 1832 (now identified as originating from Jiexiu 介休) and the manuscript dated 1711 in the collection of the library of the Institute of Literature of the Chinese Academy of Social Sciences in her collation. This latter manuscript closely follows the text of the earlier printed edition.

54. Yang Taikang and Cao Zhanmei 2006, 1091–92. The compilers of this collection have no information on the identity of the Third Lad 三郎為何神, 待考 ("more research is needed to determine the identity of the Third Lad as a god"). A local legend recorded in Anonymous 1999, 67–69, credits the foundation of the temple to Emperor Wuzong's (r. 1308–1311) fondness for a local filial son who cured his mother's blindness by licking her eyes. That filial son is described as an eldest son, so it not clear what his link to the Third Lad might be.

dreamed that Liu Bang 劉邦, the founder of the Western Han dynasty (206 BCE–6 CE), informed him that the Yellow River would be solidly frozen. When Liu Xiu dispatched the eldest of three brothers to check out the situation and that man reported that the river was flowing freely, he was immediately beheaded by Liu Xiu, and the same fate befell the second brother when he reported the true situation. The youngest brother, also ordered to go to the river, decided to lie and report that the river was solidly frozen. The delighted Liu Xiu called him a divinity, and when he led the army to the Yellow River found that it was indeed solidly frozen. But when he wanted to reward the youngest of the three brothers, it transpired that the man had already committed suicide, as he feared to be killed when Liu Xiu would find out he had lied. When Liu Xiu, once he became emperor, wanted to honor him with a temple, the eunuch dispatched for its construction mistakenly built it in Yangcheng in Shanxi, after which local farmers built a temple at the spot of his suicide in Yangcheng village in Henan, closer to the Yellow River.[55]

Perhaps even more intriguing is the fact that the Third Lad in our tale is given not two but four brothers. Modern scholars such as Ma Xisha and Che Xilun have suggested that as a pentad these gods may be comparable to other divine pentads that were revered as the Wutong 五通 (Five Powers), the Wusheng 五聖 (Five Sages), or Wuxian 五顯 (Five Manifestations). Such divinities, best known from the Jiangnan area, grant riches to their devotees, but also are very jealous; when they feel slighted by their devotees they may strike them with disasters.[56] In at least one (nineteenth-century?) manuscript version, rich man Zhang and his wife woman Yang do indeed pray for a child at a temple to the Five Sages (*wushengshen miao* 五聖神廟),[57] but in the versions of the baojuan recorded in Gansu the divinity they pray to has remained the Third Lad,[58] and he and his brothers show none of the characteristics of the southern pentads, so it may well be too rash to identify the Third Lad and his four brothers with those deities. Unfortunately, neither Ma Xisha nor Che Xilun provides any more detailed information to substantiate their suggestion.

If the Third Lad's origin is not connected to the divine pentads from the south, he may have another southern origin. Near the Jade Mountain Monastery in Jingzhou, the place where the great general Guan Yu 關羽 (d. 219) had died, there was a shrine dedicated to the veneration of the Third Lad. This

---

55. Meng Dan and Wang Guangxian 2011, 535–36.
56. On these gods, see, for instance, Cedzich 1995; Glahn 1991; Guo 2003; Lévy 1971.
57. Sawada Mizuho 1975, 295.
58. Ji Qiuyue 2019, 53–55. It should also be pointed out that whereas the five divinities that make up the Wutong, Wusheng, and Wuxian would appear to be of equal rank, the four brothers would appear to be of minor importance compared to the Third Lad.

shrine already existed in Tang dynasty times. Scholars have discussed the identity of the deity revered here, and while some believe it must be Guan Yu in person,[59] others believe it must have been his third (adopted) son, Guan Ping 關平 (d. 219). No later than the early years of the eleventh century there were two shrines on Jade Mountain, one dedicated to the worship of Guan Yu and the other to the worship of the Third Lad, now explicitly identified as Guan Ping. The divine status of Guan Yu would only continue to increase over the course of the second millennium, and Guan Ping too would become a major deity in late imperial times.[60] Whereas Guan Yu was never listed as a member of a pentad, there is a hint that Guan Ping may have had four companions. We are accustomed to paintings and statues of Guan Yu accompanied by Zhou Cang 周倉 and Guan Ping, but on an early print recovered from the ruins of Karakhoto and printed in Pingyang (often dated to the Jin dynasty but more likely dating from the Yuan), Guan Yu is surrounded by five attendants, including Guan Ping.[61] Could it be that at one time this fivesome was venerated as such? That would also explain the special position of the Third Lad among this pentad. In the absence of any supporting evidence, this can only be a hypothesis, especially as neither Guan Yu nor Guan Ping enjoys a reputation for providing children to childless couples (a task that is usually entrusted to female deities).

In view, however, of the connection of the Third Lad's brothers to the underworld (they use the City of Unjust Deaths as their private prison), the Third Lad in the *Precious Scroll of the Red Gauze* most likely can be identified with the Third Lad of Mt. Tai (Taishan Sanlang 泰山三郎), better known as Bingling gong 炳靈公 (Duke of Blazing Numinosity), the favorite third son of the Great Thearch of the Eastern Marchmount (Dongyue dadi 東嶽大帝). In Tang times, this young man appears as a wastrel who takes possession of other men's wives, but in 933 he was awarded the rank of Generalissimo of Might and Valor (Weixiong dajiangjun 威雄大將軍) after the second emperor of the Later Tang dynasty had been cured of a disease by a monk who told him that the Great Thearch had ordered him to request a title for his beloved third son. This title was raised to that of Bingling gong in 1014. This Third Lad had four brothers who only received official titles in 1099 but of a much lower rank.[62] In the *Xinbian lianxiang soushen guangji* 新編連相搜神廣記 (Newly compiled and fully illustrated: The expanded record in search of the gods) of

---

59. Haar 2017, 29.
60. Wang Jianchuan 1999, 112–14.
61. Wang Shucun, Li, and Liu 1989, pl. 2.
62. This is a summary of the various sources on Bingling gong collected by Zong Li and Liu Qun 1986, 291–94.

the Yuan dynasty and its later versions from the Ming, the title of Third Lad is even given as Zhisheng Bingling wang 至聖炳靈王 (Most Holy Prince of Blazing Numinosity).[63] Popular religious tracts would provide him with even more grandiose titles, such as "imperial lord" (*dijun* 帝君). In late imperial China, Bingling gong was widely venerated, not only as an attendant of his mighty father but also in his own right, both in temples dedicated to his father and in temples dedicated to himself. In connection with the *Precious Scroll of the Red Gauze*, it is significant to note that in the Beijing temple dedicated to the Great Thearch of the Eastern Marchmount (Dongyuemiao 東嶽廟), his third son also was venerated in the early 1930s as one of the deities "who delivered babies to their destined homes."[64]

In view of the many miracles that are performed by the Third Lad, one wonders whether the *Precious Scroll of the Red Gauze* might originally have been written in honor of this deity, very much in the manner (despite the lack of any reference to the mortal life of the Third Lad) of the *Precious Scroll of the Immortal Maiden Equal to Heaven*, which devotes two-thirds of its text to the miracles wrought by this deity. But strangely enough, once Huaxian has been sent on his way to find his father, the Third Lad drops from the tale. One would at least have expected Huaxian to pay a visit to the temple of the Third Lad on his return to his place of birth and the reunion of his family to thank the deity who had saved him from so many disasters. One wonders whether the disappearance from the text of the Third Lad may have occurred because the *Precious Scroll of the Red Gauze* shows a much stronger impact of the cult of the Unborn Old Mother than the *Precious Scroll of the Handkerchief*.[65] When woman Yang embroiders the precious curtain for the Third Lad, the pictorial program includes the Unborn Old Mother (here introduced as the Buddha's grandmother):

> She embroidered the Buddha's grandmother at the gathering at Spirit Mountain: Ever since the Unborn Old Mother has seen her children disperse she has been unable to see them again and at all times she hopes that the men and women throughout the world will come home, and she fears that when the three disasters will arrive, they will lose their

---

63. *Huitu sanjiao yuanliu soushen daquan (wai erzhong)* 1990, 483.
64. Goodrich 1964, 75. In her 1927 description of the same temple, Janet R. Ten Broeck notes that the rooms dedicated to the four brothers of Bingling gong "are kept closed and there is no sign of recent worship" (Goodrich 1964, 256).
65. Che Xilun (2009, 518) points out that in versions of the *Precious Scroll of the Red Gauze* from the Daoguang period (1821–1850) and later these references to the Unborn Old Mother are lacking. Ji Qiuyue (2019, 49–53) relates this to increased persecution of sectarian religions from the Qianlong period onward.

spiritual light and for eighty-one kalpas forever will be unable to meet with their mother again.[66]

In the ritual conclusion we read detailed instructions for the believers:

> Ask an enlightened teacher,
>   Seek out friends in the Way,
>   To know what are the Four Phenomena:
> All is vacuous emptiness;
>   The Dharma world spreads throughout,
>   Permeating the cosmos of Qian and Kun.
> The Mother carried you
>   And she gave birth to you,
>   All nine hundred and ninety thousand,
> And after eighty kalpas
>   We have arrived at the coming
>   Congregation of the Dragon-Flower.
> Arrived at this point
>   You must let go
>   And make yet another step forward:
> Cross the Dark Gate,
>   Surpass the three realms,
>   And return to your fate and your roots.
> I urge this assembly
>   Not to miss the opportunity
>   Of the great meaning from the West:
> At Maitreya's
>   Dragon-Flower Assembly
>   You'll achieve a second body of gold.[67]

And we learn that the devotees of the Unborn Old Mother will not only be reunited with her but even reenter her womb: "Board the floating boat of the Unborn to reach the shore, and the little infants will be reunited with their own mother. Once inside the mother's womb you don't have to fear the three disasters, you will join the Dragon Flower for the eighty-first kalpa, and for all eternity enjoy peace and prosperity."[68] A close reading of the text, however, suggests that these passages related to the Unborn Old Mother are isolated

---

66. Shang Lixin 2018, 81.
67. Shang Lixin 2018, 99.
68. Shang Lixin 2018, 99. This passage is also encountered in the *Precious Scroll of the Handkerchief*.

insertions that have no relation to the following or preceding text.[69] Could it be that the tale of Huaxian's separation from his parents and his efforts to be reunited with them had originally been composed in praise of the miraculous powers of the Third Lad, but that some later editor had seen in this tale a suitable allegorical vehicle for the propagation of the belief in the Unborn Old Mother and had edited the text accordingly? The Ming edition includes statements that indeed suggest that its text had passed through a number of editions.

When the *Precious Scroll, as Preached by the Buddha, of Little Huaxian: How Woman Yang as a Ghost Embroidered Red Gauze* was first introduced to the scholarly world in an article by Ma Xisha in 1986, he quoted the line following the full title to hail this work as a publication of the late thirteenth century and therefore our earliest known precious scroll.[70] This line may be translated as follows:

> Newly cut in the year Geng-Yin of the Zhiyuan reign (1290). The monk Jiren of the Yuanjue Hermitage outside the Jubao Gate of Jinling initiated the carving as a gift to the multitude. 至元庚寅新刻金陵聚寶門外 圓覺庵比丘集 仁捐眾開雕

The expression "newly cut" implies, of course, that the preserved edition was not the first printing. Such an earlier edition would seem to be implied by a few lines found following the table of contents:

> Revised and compiled at imperial behest 依旨修纂
> For distribution throughout the world 頒行天下
> On the longest day of the year in the first year of the Chongqing
>   reign, a Ren-Shen year (1212) 崇慶元年歲次壬申長至日

This date moves the original composition of the text to the early thirteenth century, if not earlier, if we assume that the text that was published at imperial behest was itself a revised version of an earlier work. The imperial court involved would be the Jürched Jin dynasty, as Chongqing was a reign period that lasted only one year during the short rule of Weishaowang 衛紹王 (r. 1209–1212). This dating also suggests that the text may have been composed in northern China.

If the text of the preserved sixteenth-century printing could indeed be identified with the text of any of these thirteenth-century editions, such a dating

---

69. Richard Shek (1999, 361) states that Ma Xisha in a private discussion agreed that these passages were late interpolations.
70. Ma Xisha 1986.

would of course have major implications for the study of Chinese religion and the study of Chinese literature, as Ma Xisha emphatically pointed out. It would imply that precious scrolls had already acquired their sixteenth-century format by the early thirteenth century, and it would imply that the cult of the Unborn Old Mother did not originate in the Ming dynasty, as is usually assumed, but was already fully developed by that same date. Both Li Shiyu and Che Xilun, however, stress the similarities of the formal features of the present text of the *Precious Scroll, as Preached by the Buddha, of Little Huaxian: How Woman Yang as a Ghost Embroidered Red Gauze* to the precious scrolls of the sixteenth century, and they reject the dates 1212 and 1290 as fakes (*weituo* 偽 托), presumably inserted to enhance the status of the text.[71] Che Xilun reads the statement concerning the monk Jiren as explaining the origin of the edition of 1290 and points out that the south gate of Nanjing (since 1933 known as the Zhonghuamen 中華門) was known as the Jubaomen 聚寶門 (Cornucopia Gate) only since the early Ming dynasty. As further proof that that name started to circulate only in the Ming, he refers to the legend of the financial contributions to the building of the present gate by the very wealthy Shen Xiu 沈秀.[72] However, the current gate was built on the same spot as the southern gate of the Song and the Yuan and is said to have received its name from the fact that it was facing Jubaoshan 聚寶山 (Mt. Cornucopia, now known as Yuhuatai 雨花台).[73] If that is so, the southern gate may well have conventionally been known as Jubaomen even before the Ming. And even if the name became common only after the foundation of the Ming, that does not automatically imply that the edition financed by the monk Jiren was the 1290 one. That could well have been the edition he used when he initiated the carving of new blocks by the end of the sixteenth century (the Yuanjue Hermitage outside the Cornucopia Gate was founded sometime during the Wanli reign period [1573–1619]).[74] Jiren may well have had his blocks carved in Nanjing, but if that is the case, the current edition may be a fourth printing, because "the gentleman in charge of books Wu Yangquan 管理書籍舍人吳仰泉" who informs us at the end of the table of contents that he "further ordered fine craftsmen to create two picture sheets and to carefully carve fine plates 再命

---

71. Che Xilun 1997, 60–62; Che Xilun 2009, 513–18. Li Shiyu (2007, 50–51) assigns the text to the middle of the Qing dynasty. Overmyer 1999, 287–89, agrees with the conclusions of Che Xilun, because he too is convinced that the cult of the Unborn Old Mother only fully emerged in the sixteenth century.
72. Che Xilun 2009, 515.
73. Ji Shijia 1981, 154–57; Wu Qingzhou 2005, 114.
74. Feng Ye 2019, 272.

良工治圖二福謹鏤佳板,"[75] identifies himself at the end of the text as "Bookseller Wu Yangquan 書林吳仰泉," opening up the possibility that the currently available *Precious Scroll, as Preached by the Buddha, of Little Huaxian: How Woman Yang as a Ghost Embroidered Red Gauze* was a commercial venture.[76]

Other precious scrolls that claim a much earlier composition date for their text than the actual date usually combine such a statement with a claim of divine revelation.[77] Such a claim is not made in any of the lines on the printing history of the *Precious Scroll, as Preached by the Buddha, of Little Huaxian: How Woman Yang as a Ghost Embroidered Red Gauze*, which stand out because of their atypical factuality. In the preface to the first series of his *Zhonghua zhenben baojuan*, Ma Xisha accepts that the presently available text is a Ming dynasty revision, but he strongly rejects Che Xilun's suggestion that the dates 1212 and 1290 are pure inventions of the Ming publisher. Like Ma, I see no reason to doubt that earlier versions of our precious scroll may have been printed in the thirteenth century. That works of prosimetric literature were printed during the Jin dynasty is proven by the preserved fragments of the *Liu Zhiyuan zhugongdiao* 劉知遠諸宮調 (All keys and modes on Liu Zhiyuan), and that such prosimetric texts could be works of considerable sophistication is proven by Dong Jieyuan's 董解元 *Xixiang ji zhugongdiao* 西廂記諸宮調 (All keys and modes on the Tale of the Western Wing) of circa 1200. Also, the involvement of the Jin dynasty court is not improbable.[78] One may see yet another proof of the interest of the Jin dynasty court in precious scrolls if indeed it was an early version of the legend of woman Huang that was translated into the Jürched language.

---

75. The text indeed includes two pages of illustration. The first is very finely produced and shows a lady leaning on the balustrade outside a second-floor window and listlessly gazing into the distance. Its relevance to the story is not immediately clear. The second page is divided into four spaces showing (1) rich man Zhang and woman Yang praying to the Third Lad; (2) woman Yang at the loom in the underworld; (3) woman You giving a beating to Huaxian; and (4) woman Yang urging Huaxian to show mercy.

76. In a personal communication, Lucille Chia informed me that Wu Yangquan most likely was a Huizhou bookseller who was active in Nanjing. The surname Wu was quite common among those active in publishing in Huizhou during the Ming. Some of these persons also opened shops in Nanjing, advertising themselves as *shulin* 書林 (bookseller).

77. Dudbridge 2004, 49–50, 83–84.

78. The genre would continue to be patronized by royalty in later times too. The 1372 copy of the early precious scroll on Mulian was associated with the surviving Yuan court, and the 1440 copy of the same text was donated by an imperial consort of the Ming. We know that in the sixteenth century, palace eunuchs and princesses, as well officials in some cases, sponsored the publication of precious scrolls. In the final years of the seventeenth century, the *Precious Scroll of the Immortal Maiden Equal to Heaven* was published with the support of the military governor of Gansu, and in the eighteenth century the royal court in Vietnam sponsored the printing of an edition of the *Precious Scroll of Incense Mountain*.

With each new edition of the *Precious Scroll of the Red Gauze* the text may have been revised (as happened to the various versions of the precious scroll on Mulian), and if monk Jiren lived during the Ming rather than the Yuan, he would appear to be the most likely candidate for the revision of the text that resulted in its present shape. It seems more improbable to assume such a role for the publisher Wu Yangquan, even if he may have tried to increase the attractiveness of his product by the addition of illustrations. If the monk Jiren can indeed be identified with the "monk" (*nazi* 訥子) who presents himself in the text as its compiler, who "exhausted [his] mind in its collection and completion," he may have turned an earlier version of the text into a typical sixteenth-century precious scroll by adapting the format where needed (for instance, by a formal division into chapters and the inclusion of songs at the opening of each chapter); he may have added the passages on the Unborn Old Mother at the same time. If we hold him responsible for this makeover, the repeated insistence on the longing of the mother for her son and of the son for his mother in the opening songs of the chapters becomes more understandable.

* * *

The *Precious Scroll of Woman Huang*, the *Precious Scroll of the Red Gauze*, and the *Precious Scroll of the Handkerchief* share many common elements. Despite the different historical settings (the Han, the Tang, and the Song), the social setting is the same: the families of wealthy businessmen. The husbands of woman Yang and woman Zhang are both designated as *yuanwai* 員外 (supernumerary official), a term that by the Ming dynasty had become a common designation for the heads of wealthy families without any connection to the bureaucracy. Even if such families sent their sons to school, the first expectation was that these sons would inherit the family business and maintain the family's wealth. This family wealth allowed their womenfolk (whether daughters and wives) to indulge in their pious passions, such as the acquisition of pious books and the construction of private Buddha chapels. As businessmen, their husbands and fathers also would not necessarily have harbored the strong ideological opposition against Buddhism to which a Confucian gentleman was expected to subscribe. The business interests of these rich men explained their frequent absences from home, whether they had to collect outstanding loans or decided to go on a trading trip. Even woman Huang's husband, who is described as a butcher, probably is more like a magnate in the meat industry, as he is said at one moment to leave on a trip to Shandong to buy pigs. These shorter absences from home allow for the festering of conflicts between wives and concubines, and second wives and children of the first wife, which could easily degenerate into violence. The butcher Zhao Lingfang would appear to be an exception in that he did not remarry upon his wife's demise, sparing his children the fate woman Huang herself had suffered in her youth in some versions of the legend.

In this world of intense belief and scoffing agnosticism, the gods and buddhas have to intervene in order to show their power. Stories often start with the miraculous birth of a child to elderly parents, and throughout these tales, gods intervene to assist those who are good and pious and punish those who are evil and mean. But the gods usually take their time before they intervene. They also may take the souls of their devotees to the underworld years before their time. While the *Precious Scroll of the Red Gauze* highlights the frequent actions of the Third Lad, the other precious scrolls in this volume have a larger cast of gods. By their piety, both woman Huang and Zhang Suzhen induce the bodhisattva Guanyin to manifest herself. The Unborn Old Mother is appealed to in the concluding sections of the *Precious Scroll of Woman Huang*, the *Precious Scroll of the Red Gauze*, and the *Precious Scroll of the Handkerchief*. But the Unborn Old Mother does not interfere in the action of the stories. It is primarily in the concluding sections of these three precious scrolls that their audiences are urged to place their faith in the saving powers of this divinity who longs to gather all her children in her womb.

The *Precious Scroll, as Preached by the Buddha, of Little Huaxian: How Woman Yang as a Ghost Embroidered Red Gauze*

Newly cut in the year Geng-Yin of the Zhiyuan reign (1290). The monk Jiren of the Yuanjue Hermitage outside the Jubao Gate of Jinling initiated this carving as a gift to the multitude.

I. The King of the Great Tang Rules the World
II. Rich Man Zhang and Woman Yang Seek a Son and Heir
III. The Left Golden Lad Is Born in the Family of Rich Man Zhang
IV. In the Temple Rich Man Zhang and his Wife Express Their Thanks to the Deities
V. Her Ladyship Woman Yang Embroiders the Red Gauze Curtain
VI. Woman Yang Embroiders the Dragon Palace and the Storehouse of the Ocean
VII. The Rich Man Takes His Wife and His Son along to Present the Red Gauze Precious Curtain
VIII. The Vexations of Her Ladyship Woman Yang in the Underworld
IX. Woman Kang Visits the Rich Man as Matchmaker
X. Little Huaxian Longs for His Mother
XI. Woman You Marries Rich Man Zhang
XII. Rich Man Zhang Gives Woman You, His Evil Wife, a Beating
XIII. Woman You Heats the Wok to Harm the Little Boy
XIV. The Rich Man Comes Home and Woman You Covers Things Up

XV. Woman You Does In Little Boy Huaxian Using Poison
XVI. After Woman You Has Mistakenly Killed Her Son, She Lodges an Accusation
XVII. After the Autumn Assizes Little Huaxian Is about to Be Beheaded
XVIII. In an Abandoned Kiln Little Huaxian Longs for His Father and Mother
XIX. Little Huaxian Visits the Prison, and Father and Son Are Reunited
XX. To the Beat of *Lotus Flowers Fall* Little Huaxian Begs for Food and Saves His Father
XXI. Little Huaxian Becomes Prince Consort and Saves His Father from Prison
XXII. The Rich Man, His Wife, the Princess, and the Prince Consort Are Reunited

Revised and compiled at Imperial behest
For distribution throughout the world
On the longest day of the year in the first year of the Chongqing reign, a Ren-Shen year (1212)

The gentleman in charge of books Wu Yangquan
Further ordered fine craftsmen to create two picture sheets and to carefully carve fine plates. May those who observe them treasure them.

The *Precious Scroll*, as Preached by the Buddha, of Little Huaxian: How Woman Yang as a Ghost Embroidered Red Gauze

The Red Gauze Precious Scroll
Descended to the dharma world:[1]
A bodhisattva reborn on earth came down from the heavenly palace.
Because of her little boy
She could not find any peace:
Mother and son were torn apart.

Hail to the Bodhisattva Mahasattva who saves from sufferings and disasters! (the community repeats this three times)[2]

---

1. The dharma world or Dharmadhatu here refers to the physical universe. At other places the term may refer to the unifying underlying spiritual reality regarded as the ground or cause of all things.
2. Bodhisattva Mahasattva is often used in reference to the bodhisattva Guanyin.

> The bodhisattva reborn on earth descended from heaven
> To save us, men and women, from the dust of suffering.
> Illusionary bodies, fake phenomena, encounter disasters:
> Barely escaping from death we emerge from immersion.

Hail to the Three Treasures of Buddha, Dharma, and Sangha of the Past, the Present, and the Future that, Utterly Void, Pervade the dharma worlds!

> The unsurpassable and unfathomable subtle and wonderful Dharma
> Is rarely encountered in a hundred thousands of millions of kalpas.[3]
> Now I today have seen it and heard it, and can receive and uphold it,
> I desire to understand the Tathāgata's true and substantial meaning.[4]

I have learned that the Buddhas of the three worlds and the bodhisattvas of all heavens admonish us men because we do not realize that life and death are all the original source of the Buddhas and that mountains and rivers and the whole earth are the dharma bodies of the bodhisattvas and the Dharma Body of the Buddha pervading the hundred times thousand times ten thousand times thousand worlds, in which the men of this world are reborn and transformed according to their karmic causes. Because all living beings are confused and disordered and don't believe the Proper Dharma and have lost their root source, I urge all monks and nuns, clerics and laymen and all people of the four classes that they have to believe that the Buddhas of the three worlds day and night circulate to save and ferry across[5] all living beings.

> For the sake of mercy, for the sake of mercy, for the sake of great mercy
> I entrust my fate to each and all of the Buddha, Dharma, and Sangha
>   of the ten directions!
> May the Dharma Wheel, constantly turning,[6] ferry across all living beings!

I have heard that when man is born between heaven and earth, his fate is entrusted to Yin and Yang, while poverty and wealth, nobility and baseness are all the result of a person's cultivation [in a former life]. So I admonish the people presently alive: You must have heard that the sutras teach that Śākyamuni abandoned the palace and that Emperor Wu of the Liang obtained

---

3. A kalpa is the unimaginably long period between the formation of a world system and its destruction.

4. The Tathāgatha refers to the Buddha.

5. To achieve enlightenment is often compared to reaching the other shore of a river. The message of Buddhism may serve as the ferry or boat that ferries the believers across.

6. The Dharma Wheel (or Wheel of the Law) refers to the teachings of the Buddha that can crush all evil and all opposition and will continue to roll forever.

the position of king after he had donated his bamboo hat.[7] If one doesn't plant in spring, one will not harvest in fall. If you practice goodness, you will achieve good results; if you practice evil, you will achieve evil results. If you fight and struggle with people, you will immediately suffer retribution. So I admonish you, men and women: Human life passes as quickly as a flare of lightning or a spark from a stone, so don't wait or tarry, but quickly start cultivating yourself and upholding [the Dharma]. Birth, old age, sickness, and death are like a tangle of illusions: morning or night is unfathomable,[8] so don't fight for fame and struggle over profit. The men and women of the whole earth don't realize anymore that being born and passing away are the root source of the Buddha, and if you have lost your true origin, it is difficult to recognize your home and your remorse will be without cause. Alas!

> If here in the present you're clear, truly clear,
> Then you will not be off by a hair upon death.

As soon as the Precious Scroll of the Red Gauze is opened,
All Buddhas and bodhisattvas descend to attend the recital.
Dragons and devas and other divinities, revered like stupas,
Will protect and guard this gathering, forever imperishable.
  I urge all you men and women who have come to attend
To quickly practice self-cultivation and develop goodness.
If you refuse to believe the good words by which I urge you,
You cannot avoid upon death to appear before King Yama.[9]
  Hundreds and thousands of theories only pulverize the heart,
And all those nonsensical objections make a heretical school.
The clear distinction of orthodox and heretical generates life,
But those deluded people throughout the world have no clue.
  This cleric clearly ferries you across the thousands of causes:
The Buddha protects you, Heaven supports you in your house.
Here on earth one cannot tell the truth clearly just by words,
So I clearly point it out, showing it up there in central Heaven.

The Ancients and the Gods
Never depart from the root:
To mystery they add another mystery.

---

7. According to Buddhist teaching, the source of all suffering is attachment to worldly goods; accordingly, one of the greatest virtues is generosity and liberality, the willingness to donate one's possessions (including one's relatives and one's body).
8. That is, the moment of death will be unpredictable.
9. King Yama is the highest ruler of the underworld. The souls of the deceased will appear before him to be judged according to their sins and virtues, which have all been carefully recorded by his staff.

Containing a wonderful body,
It is a heaven beyond heaven.
If you pass one day and night
In that unborn precious land,
Five hundred years have passed on earth.

> Though this is clearly explained,
> Men and women don't grasp it.
> Miss your chance face to face,
> And you'll never get another.

I. The King of the Great Tang Rules the World

[Shangxiaolou][10]

The Scroll of Red Gauze has been left to us by the Buddhas,
And I, this monk, have exhausted my mind in its collection and
    completion:
Rich man Zhang and his son and his mother encountered problems
    without end, without rest.
When the left golden lad[11] was born on earth he met with disaster,
But the divinity came to his rescue.
The Buddhas are present in the human realm
But we are caught in the cycle of rebirth—
Who is able to see through this state of affairs?

[Plain prose] This is my humble advice to all men and women: When you are born in this world, you cannot have everything. If you have a son, you may lack fortune and riches, but when you have no son, you may be very rich: it is impossible to have everything.

Now let me tell you that during the Tang dynasty there lived a certain rich man Zhang. He had no sons or grandsons. One day when he went with some other men to a dinner party, he saw as they were walking along some students greeting them. When they greeted the other rich men, they respectfully made a deep bow, but when they greeted rich man Zhang, they only did so perfunctorily and insolently. Rich man Zhang was upset, and grasping the students he asked them, "We are all equally rich men. But when you greet the other rich men, you make a deep bow, so why do you only perform half a bow when

---

   10. The names of the song tunes are left untranslated. While these names originally may have had some connection to the contents of the song, that connection was lost at an early date.
   11. Deities are often depicted with a young servant boy to their left and a young servant girl to their right.

greeting me?" These students said with one voice, "These other rich men have sons who are our fellow students who are our devoted friends. You don't have children, that's why we ignore you." When the rich man heard this, he silently bowed his head and went back home.

>When his wife was welcoming rich man Zhang,
>She saw that tears were coursing down his face.

When rich man Zhang
    Arrived back home,
        His heart was filled with vexation;
Deeply wounded at heart,
    He felt quite dispirited
        And let his tears flow profusely:
If you have great riches
    And sons and daughters,
        All people will show you respect,
But if you are wealthy
    Without sons and daughters,
        You are not even counted a man!
Now he had a wife,
    Named woman Yang,
        Who stepped forward and asked,
"For what reason
    Are you today
        Feeling at a loss and bewildered?"
When the rich man told her,
    And his wife knew the reason,
        The two of them felt quite vexed:
"Once we are old,
    Without any children,
        Everything will all turn to nothing.
When a disaster strikes us
    Or we are laid down by illness,
        Who will know the pains we suffer?
This whole household
    Of over a hundred
        Will treat us like utter strangers.
I get up before dawn,
    Sleep only till midnight,
        Collecting interest on my loans,

But when I cannot
    Breathe anymore,
        It will only be one rasping sound,
And who will own
    These millions of cash
        Without any sons or daughters?
Part will be stolen,
    Part carried off—
        Frittered away till nothing is left!"
When his wife heard
    What her husband said,
        She was deeply troubled and said,
"It is all my fault
    That I didn't conceive
        And that we don't have children.
If at thirty
    You don't have children,
        People will not show any respect;
If at forty
    You don't have children,
        Even your relatives will shun you.
If at fifty
    You don't have children,
        You are without any descendants;
Once you are sixty,
    You're a tree above a ravine—
        The dead roots washed by water.
If one counts further,
    You cannot be sure
        Of the day of today or tomorrow.[12]
Since early youth
    We've sought fame and profit,
        Vainly passing the days of our life."

Woman Yang suddenly understood,
She was quite smart and intelligent,
"My husband, please set your worries aside!
Now in front of the drum tower,

---

12. Of the day of one's death.

Right at the central crossing,
Is the temple of the Third Lad,
A sage deity that has great numinous power.
The two of us should go there,
And pray for a son, seeking a clear answer!"

> Woman Yang was extremely intelligent,
> And made a vow, seeking a son and heir.
> The rich man too was sincere and devout,
> So Heaven sent down the left golden lad.

II. Rich Man Zhang and Woman Yang Seek a Son and Heir

[Langtaosha]

Woman Yang deliberated with her husband,
"If we also promise a pig and a sheep,
His Lordship must be moved to send down a son.
We will refashion all divine statues,
Renew the canopies,
And brightly paint the carved beams."
Rich man Zhang arrived at the temple hall
And sincerely prayed to the Third Lad.
He came to seek a son or a daughter,
And offered a pig and a sheep.
The Third Lord was absent, away on a trip,
So who dared take on this request?

[Plain prose] Tell that rich man Zhang and woman Yang gathered the fruits and other offerings and arrived inside the temple. There they lit incense and bowed down, asking the Third Lad for a son. When they had finished their prayers, it happened that the divinity was not there, so the big ghosts and small ghosts, the underworld judges and minor gods didn't dare make a promise. Before his departure rich man Zhang made yet another vow: If he would be granted one son or half a daughter, he would renovate the temple and redecorate the gold statue. Thereupon the two of them returned home—and no more of them.

Now tell that his Lordship the Third Lad on returning from his meeting of celestial officials noticed that the offering table was filled with sacrificial goods, including pork and lamb, so he asked his ghostly underlings, "Where does this come from?" These replied, "Rich man Zhang and his wife came here together to seek a child, and because Your Lordship was not here, none of us dared make any promise." When the Third Lad heard this, he ordered the underworld judges to make an inquiry who could be dispatched to be reborn in that family. The underworld judges reported, "There is a golden lad in the superior realm who broke an incense burner. He has been sentenced to descend to earth, but has not yet been sent down." The Third Lad then said, "So let's give this golden lad to the Zhang family as their son."

        The ghostly underlings then led the left golden lad
        To the Zhang family to be reborn as their one son.

The ghostly underlings
   Led the left golden lad
      To be reborn below on earth,
And in an instant
   They had arrived
      Outside the rich man's gate.
On entering her room
   They said to the lady,
      "Woman Yang, do not fear:
You asked for,
   We bring you
      This little boy as your son."
The ghostly underlings
   Had the left golden boy
      Enter the shell of her womb;
The lady so carried
   The boy in her womb,
      And the ghosts then returned.
Early next morning
   That woman Yang
      Told the rich man her husband,
"This last night
   I had a dream
      And as midnight was sounded,
I saw in my dream
   A ghost who led
      A little boy to my side,
And he told me,
   This is the son and heir,
      The descendant you prayed for."

When rich man Zhang
    Had heard these words,
        He thanked Heaven and Earth,
And promptly bowed down
    Before the divine statues
        To express his thanks to the gods.

The golden crow sinks in the west,
And the jade hare rises in the east,
Urging forward heaven and earth and mankind.[13]
In the wink of the eye
The time had passed,
And woman Yang
Gave birth to a son:
Soon grown to three years,
Painstakingly cared for by his father and mother.

        The rich man had prayed for a son;
        Woman Yang gave birth to an heir.
        Soon he had grown to three years,
        When disaster struck once again.

III. The Left Golden Lad Is Born in the Family of Rich Man Zhang

[Miandaxu]
The rich man was quite happy,
Woman Yang was never at ease:
Day and night she had no peace,
Always flustered and in a panic.
She could catch no sleep,
And always felt anxious,
Constantly flustered and worried
That some accident might occur,
And when a disaster threatened,
She seemed to have lost her mind
As she fervently prayed to the gods passing through the air!

---

13. The golden crow inhabits the sun, and the jade hare inhabits the moon.

[Plain prose] Tell that woman Yang each day never felt at ease, whether sitting or lying down. When she saw that her son had grown to the age of three years with clear eyebrows and bright eyes, a picture to behold, she gave the little boy therefore the name of Huaxian—but no more about that.[14]

Just tell that the Third Lad in his temple one day suddenly remembered rich man Zhang and his wife. "How insolent! You and your wife asked me for a son or a daughter and I had the left golden lad be reborn in your family. He is now three, but I have never seen you come and thank me!" He then ordered his ghostly underlings, "Go to the house of rich man Zhang and bring me the true soul of the little boy." These ghostly underlings didn't dare tarry, and as one breeze of fresh air they arrived at the gate of rich man Zhang and stole the true soul of the little boy—but no more about that.

> The rich man mourns his little son, as knives gouge his lungs;
> His wife carries him in her arms, her heart pierced by swords.

The father cried out,
   "My dear little boy,
      You are burying your father's fate!
You abandon your parents,
   Leave your father and mother,
      Cutting off all love and attachment!
Looking on you
   Your parents had hoped
      You would care for us in our dotage,
But now in dying
   You have left us—
      All our efforts have been in vain!"
His mother cried,
   "Whether day or night,
      I looked after you each hour again.
I breastfed you for three years,
   Slept in my dirtied clothes,
      Devoting all my energy to your care.
We hired a wet nurse
   To carry you in her arms,
      Afraid that you might be frightened;[15]

---

14. Huaxian means "transformed immortal."
15. "Fright" is often listed as a cause of childhood diseases.

Walking before and behind,
   We as your father and mother
      Followed you anxiously around.
During the summer heat
   Your mother would
      Cool you by constantly waving a fan;
During the winter frost
   Your mother would
      Carry you in her arms to keep you warm.
Your mother raised you
   For these three years,
      Never daring to put you down,
And once she fell asleep,
   She still was dreaming
      She was holding her boy in her arms.
But now today
   Your life has ended
      Because of some unknown reason;
In vain, it turns out,
   Has been all my suffering—
      My love for you will be my death!"
And she cried out,
   "My dear little boy,
      If you indeed will have passed away,
I will kill myself
   And together with you
      Go and meet with the Yama lords!"[16]

Woman Yang was shaking,
Her husband was frightened:
They were scared out of their minds.
The time allowed no delay,
They had offended the gods.
They returned to the temple
And there fervently implored
His Lordship the Third Lad
To save their dear little boy.

---

16. Upon death the souls of the deceased have to appear before the ten courts of the underworld to be judged. These ten judges are often collectively designated as the Yama lords or Yama kings.

> The rich man, in tears and disconsolate,
> Quickly slaughtered a pig and a sheep.
> Once again he made a vow to the god,
> Praying that he might save their boy.

IV. Rich Man Zhang and His Wife in the Temple Express Their Thanks to the Deities

[Yijiangfeng]
They prayed to the gods,
"Please take pity on us—
We will have no children!"
Their tears coursed down.
Killing a pig and a sheep
They sacrificed these to the gods,
"Your Sagely Lordship, you must know,
You must know
That I will embroider a precious curtain
To present to you
If you release my son and return his soul."

[Plain prose] Tell that woman Yang knelt down in front of the temple of His Lordship the Third Lad and piteously prayed to him to release the soul of her little boy. She promised to His Lordship to embroider for him a precious curtain of red gauze which she would present to him to cover him from the cold and protect him against the heat, to ward off the dust and block the wind. When she had finished her prayer, she bowed, expressed her thanks, and left—but no more about that.

Now tell that when His Lordship the Third Lad had been promised by woman Yang that she would embroider a precious curtain of red gauze, he returned his soul to the little boy—but no more about that.

When the rich man and his wife saw that their little boy really had come back to life, they were overjoyed, and she said, "I have promised today to embroider a precious curtain of red brocade. My dear husband, please go and buy four pieces of red gauze and two pieces of blue gauze, as well as all kinds of colored silk thread, so I can start to do the embroidery."

> At a good hour she started to embroider the red gauze curtain;
> On an auspicious day she set to work, giving it her best effort.

She embroidered the thousands,
   Even the millions and billions,
      The myriads of images of the Dark Welkin;
She embroidered the Jade Emperor,
   Who is the great theocrat Zhang,
      Ruling and governing the celestial officials.
She embroidered the Spirit Peak[17]
   And its great gathered congregation
      Of hundreds of thousands of men and devas;
She embroidered the Old Buddha
   In charge of the Three Teachings
      And the ordinations of the thousand Buddhas.
She embroidered the Three Teachings,
   The Buddha, the Dharma and the Sangha,
      The Old Lord as well as the Master Confucius;
She embroidered devas and dragons
   As well as the eight kinds of beings,[18]
      And the assembled Buddhas and revered gods.
She embroidered the eastern region,
   The element Wood at the node Jia-Yi,
      The ancient ancestor who welcomes spring;[19]
She embroidered the southern region,
   The element Fire at the node Bing-Ding,
      Which in dark mystery operates as a divinity.
She embroidered the western region,
   The element Metal at the node Geng-Xin:
      In the center she embroidered the Jade Ancestor;
She embroidered the northern region,
   The element Water at the node Ren-Kui,
      That following its cultivation is greatly renowned.

---

17. The Spirit Peak is the place where the Buddha is said to have preached many of his sutras, for huge audiences of deities and humans.

18. The eight kinds of beings are the eight classes of divine beings and humans that in many sutras make up the audience of the Buddha when preaching.

19. In traditional Chinese cosmology each of the Five Directions (east, west, north, south, and central) is associated with one of the Five Phases (wood, metal, fire, water, and earth). Each of the Five Directions is also associated with one of the sixty two-character combinations made up of the ten single characters that make up the Heavenly Stems and the twelve single characters that make up the Earthly Branches.

She embroidered the central position,
> The element Earth at the node Wu-Ji,
>> With its triple body and its fourfold wisdom,

And the Wheel-Turning King[20]
> Who operates universally
>> Throughout the great earth and the cosmos.

She embroidered the heavens,
> Thirty-three their number in total,
>> Of which the central heaven doesn't move;

She embroidered the five planets,
> As well as the four Dippers,[21]
>> Brightly depicted and clearly distinguished.

She embroidered Heaven and Earth
> Together with Yin and Yang,
>> The emptiness of Li and the fullness of Kan;[22]

She embroidered the Eight Trigrams
> With their broken and unbroken lines
>> That oppose each other, engender each other.

She embroidered the Great Yang
> And its circulating golden crow—
>> When Yang returns, Yin will gain body;

She embroidered the Great Yin
> And its Jade Hare that circulates—
>> When Yin returns, Yang will be born.[23]

She embroidered Mañjuśrī[24]
> As that bodhisattva descends
>> Miraculously manifesting his true light;

---

20. Cankravartin (Wheel-Turning King) is the designation of a universal ruler in South Asian tradition. The title is often used in reference to the Buddha.

21. The "four Dippers" are the four main stars in the Northern Dipper (Ursa Major), all divinities in their own right.

22. Yin and Yang are the two contrasting and complementary powers that in their mutual waxing and waning produce the cosmos and all living beings in it. "Yang" originally referred to the sunny side of a hill and "Yin" to its shady backside, but in due time they came to stand for active and receptive, male and female. Li and Kan are two of the Eight Trigrams, Li representing Fire and Kan representing Water. When paired, the Eight Trigrams constitute the sixty-four hexagrams of the *Book of Changes*.

23. The Great Yang refers to the sun, the Great Yin to the moon. The sun is inhabited by a three-legged crow; the moon is inhabited by a hare that pounds the herbs of immortality.

24. Mañjuśrī is the bodhisattva of wisdom. He is often depicted riding a blue elephant. Samatabhadra is a bodhisattva who is acclaimed as the perfection of good deeds and spiritual practice; his mount is a white elephant. Manjusri and Samantabhadra are often depicted to the right and the left of the Buddha.

She embroidered Samantabhadra
    While producing his holy water
        That continues to stream through eternity.
She embroidered the Three Inklings
    As well as the Four Mighty Currents
        And the Twenty-Eight Lunar Lodges;[25]
She embroidered the Three Purities,
    As well as the Eleven Dazzlers
        And the Twelve Palace Hours.[26]
She embroidered Spring and Summer
    Together with Autumn and Winter
        And the Twenty-Four Solar Terms;[27]
She embroidered the years and months,
    As well as the days and the hours,
        Passing through the palace stars.[28]
She embroidered the four seasons
    Together with the eight annual nodes[29]
        And the seventy-two five-day weeks;
She embroidered the celestial bureaucrats
    As well as all the earthly bureaucrats
        And the lord of men in this cosmos.
She embroidered high and low,
    The eighty-four thousand
        Miraculous sights hidden in mystery;
She embroidered the ten directions[30]
    As well as the eight thousand,
        Shimmering and gleaming throughout.

When she had finished the heavenly palaces,
She turned to embroidering the human realm:

---

25. The Three Inklings refer to the three dates established as the beginning of the year by the first three dynasties (Xia, Yin, and Zhou). The Four Mighty Currents are the Long River (Yangzi), the Yellow River, the Huai, and the Ji. The Twenty-Eight Lodges are a selected number of constellations that are observed at certain times of the year due south at dawn or dusk.

26. The Three Purities are the highest deities in the Daoist pantheon. The sun, the moon, and the five visible planets are known as the Seven Dazzlers. The meaning of "Palace Hours" is unclear to me.

27. The solar year was divided into twenty-four periods (nodes), each with its own name.

28. The meaning of "palace stars" escapes me.

29. The eight annual nodes refer to the first days of the four seasons, the vernal and autumnal equinoxes, as well as the shortest day and the longest day.

30. The four cardinal directions, the intermediate directions, and high and low.

The ten thousand phenomena were all embroidered.
The four kinds of creatures on the six paths;[31]
The ancestral Buddhas and the root sources;
The mountains and rivers of the whole earth
With its fruits and trees, woods and streams:
Worlds as many as the drops in the Ganges
Were embroidered all in each minute detail.

> She embroidered the scenes of the heavenly palace
> And then turned to embroidering the world below.
> When all things had been completely embroidered,
> The Dharma King had been robbed of his colors.[32]

V. Her Ladyship Woman Yang Embroiders the Red Gauze Curtain

[Shanpoyang]

Woman Yang fully embroidered the palace of heaven,
In all its miraculous true features.
"I pray you, Your Lordship,
To kindly forgive, to kindly release my dear little boy."
Overcome by a searing sadness
She keenly embroidered the precious curtain of red gauze,
Embroidering till heart-broken,
Afraid something might come in between.
Her tears kept coursing down:
Because of her child she met with misfortune.
"When will I be able to finish?
Only then can I cherish some hope.
The household chores are left unattended
Because I don't dare slacken one moment."
Her sufferings were unbearable,
Her sufferings were unbearable,
But in her heart she still thought,

---

31. Living creatures are classified into four kinds according to their manner of birth: from the womb, from an egg, from moisture, or by magic. Upon death they are reborn on the six paths of rebirth (as a god, as a human being, as an animal, as a hungry ghost, etc.) depending on the karma they have accumulated during their lifetime.
32. The Dharma King is yet another title of the Buddha.

"My sufferings may be unbearable,
But I'll never dare blame Heaven."

[Plain prose] Tell that Her Ladyship woman Yang embroidered the Heavenly Palace and the ten thousand phenomena of the Dark Welkin, the planets and asterisms in heaven in all degrees of the sky, and the Buddhas of the three worlds of past[, present], and future. She embroidered the Buddha's grandmother at the gathering at Spirit Mountain: Ever since the Unborn Old Mother has seen her children disperse, she has been unable to see them again, and at all times she hopes that the men and women throughout the world will come home, and she fears that when the three disasters[33] arrive, they will lose their spiritual light and for eighty-one kalpas forever will be unable to meet with their mother again.

When she had embroidered the ten thousand images
of the heavenly palace,
She turned to embroidering the four classes of creatures
in the human realm.

She embroidered unicorns,
　Roaring lions and elephants,
　　Wolves and dholes, tigers and leopards;
She embroidered camels and donkeys,
　Water buffaloes as well as horses,
　　The running animals in their flocks and herds.
She embroidered pigs and sheep,
　As well as cats and dogs,
　　Muskdeer, roes, and little muntjacs;
She embroidered swans in the sky,
　As well as wild ducks on the ground,
　　And the freezing geese flowing ever higher.
She embroidered immortal cranes,
　As well as aged cormorants
　　With black partridges and white storks;
She embroidered mynahs
　As well as parrots
　　And grey falcons and yellow orioles.
She embroidered mandarin ducks
　As well as little ducklings
　　And egrets that stand at guard;

---

33. The destruction of our world at the end of a kalpa by fire, water, and wind.

She embroidered freezing crows
    Together with elderly ravens,
        As well as intelligent magpies.[34]
She embroidered speckled pigeons
    As well as flying squirrels,
        And birds on paired wings and their dresses.[35]
She embroidered field sparrows
    As well as yellow tits,
        And fountain owls and love birds.[36]
She embroidered swallows
    As well as house sparrows
        And the golden rooster that announces dawn;
She embroidered ducks and geese
    As well as yellow little chicks,
        And nightjars that turns into demons.[37]
She embroidered sandflies,
    Creatures of every kind,
        And francolins that can whistle;
She embroidered quails
    As well as grasshoppers
        And butterflies and dragonflies.
She embroidered phoenix couples,
    The rulers of the realm of birds
        From the south all the way to the north.
Heaven, earth and man
    Were all contained within
        A single body that encompassed all.

When she had embroidered all creatures born from a womb
She embroidered those dragons that are born from moisture,
Their palaces below the sea and all their wealthy treasures;
The dragon lord and the dragon mother,
The dragon sons and dragon grandsons,
The dragon king and his crown prince,
The dragon girls and their palace ladies,

---

34. Magpies are called intelligent because they are believed to be able to tell the future, especially the return of a loved one.
35. Translation tentative.
36. Translation tentative.
37. Translation tentative.

And the five hundred poison-dragons
That roil the River and stir up the Ocean, swaying the cosmos.

> The rivers and lakes all flow into the storehouse ocean,
> The names of the fishes are without measure or number.
> Generated from moisture there never will be any ending;
> The myriads of creatures descended from Heaven above.

VI. Woman Yang Embroiders the Dragon Palace and the Storehouse of the Ocean

[Pangzhuangtai]
Deeply grieved she sighed,
"When will I be done embroidering and can I be free?"
Clearly she had been embroidering for over a year,
And woman Yang was so tired she hardly looked human.
When she rashly made her vow, it seemed no big deal,
But it was clearly recorded in the registers of the gods.
For the sake of her son
She exhausted herself;
And only after three years
Had she completed her job.

[Plain prose] Tell that woman Yang had embroidered the heavenly palaces and the offices in the earth, and that she had also embroidered the human realm here below, the wide earth with its mountains and streams, its grasses and trees and gardens and groves, its flying birds and running beasts, its fishes and turtles and crabs and shrimps, and its rice and hemp and bamboo and reeds. She had also embroidered the four kinds of creatures on the six paths—those born from the womb, those born from an egg, those born from moisture, and those born through magic. She had also embroidered east and west, the four borders, and up and down. She had also embroidered all kinds of fruits, gourds and cucumbers, vegetables and pulses. She had completely embroidered the worlds as innumerable as the water drops in the Ganges below the sky, with all their myriads of creatures. It took three years before she was satisfied.

> Woman Yang had been engaged in embroidering for three full years;
> Only on this day the work was completed so she could thank Heaven.

> Woman Yang had made a vow with true sincerity
> To embroider a precious curtain, a gift for the god.

It displayed the full extent of three thousand worlds,
It gathered and contained the void of Great Vacuity.
This precious curtain of red gauze was not a trifle:
It protected against cold and chill, warded off dust.
When hung up, it brightly shone and clearly showed
All of heaven and earth, fully without any omission!
Woman Yang clearly possessed supernatural talents:
Her nimble hands and smart mind were so capable.
At long last her project eventually was completed:
During three years of hard work she never wavered.

The rich man was happy
And his wife was pleased
Now today her work was completed.
She packed it and delivered it
For the salvation of her child.
They killed a pig and a sheep
And so went to burn incense:
The vow fulfilled, a sacrifice
To Heaven and Earth and all divinities.

        The rich man and his wife
        Took along their little boy
        And all three came to the temple
        To make offerings and burn incense.

VII. The Rich Man Takes His Wife and His Son along to Present the Red Gauze Precious Curtain

[Langtaosha]

The rich man together with his wife
Took the little boy along
And came to the temple to bow to the gods.
Today the project was completed,
The vow was fulfilled,
And all was clearly to be seen.
The precious curtain equaled celestial palaces,
It gleamed with a glow from inside
And the innumerable worlds were all found therein.

Warm in winter, cool in summer, it had no equal:
Cold nor heat could penetrate.

[Plain prose] After the rich man with his wife and son had hung up the precious curtain, they went home—no more about them.

Now tell that His Lordship the Third Lad told the other gods not to disperse, and invited the Eldest Lad, the Second Lad, the Fourth Lad, and the Fifth Lad to join him for a banquet to appreciate the precious curtain of red gauze. After a while, the four gods had all arrived, and when they saw the precious curtain they liked it more and more. While drinking their wine, the Eldest Lad and the Second Lad said, "Third Brother, you gave the left golden lad to rich man Zhang as his son, and when he had grown to the age of three you took the true soul of the boy back to this temple because they had never thanked you. This upset woman Yang and so she promised you this precious curtain of red silk that hangs here after it took her three years to embroider it. We cannot allow you to be the only one to enjoy it." The Third Lad was upset and repeatedly said, "Dear elder brothers, woman Yang is alive and kicking, let her embroider four more curtains." The Eldest Lad said, "Arrest her soul to be released when she will have finished embroidering four more curtains." The Third Lad dispatched his ghostly underlings to fetch her soul.

> Hearing this order, the ghostly underlings don't dare tarry:
> They arrest woman Yang to take her to the realm of shade.

The two ghostly underlings
    Entered the door of her room
        To arrest and fetch woman Yang.
When the lady saw them,
    She lost all color because
        Her gall was shaken, her heart scared.
The two ghostly underlings
    Said to woman Yang,
        "There is no need to be so afraid.
We come to fetch you,
    But you're not destined to die
        And will not meet with King Yama.
His Lordship the Third Lad
    Commissions you to go
        And embroider precious curtains:

When after twelve years
   You will have finished four,
      He'll release you so you may revive."
The woman pleaded,
   But the two underlings
      Said, "No embroidering in this world!
There's no need to plead,
   Now just come with us,
      We'll quickly set out on the journey."
When they had spoken,
   They took out a rope
      With which she was tied—no escape!
So woman Yang,
   Flustered and flurried,
      Knelt down on the floor in the dust.
She prayed these ghosts
   To show some mercy
      And wait there for only a little while;
She addressed her husband
   And personally instructed him
      To take good care of her dear little boy.
So she cried out,
   "My dear husband,
      I am in this instant bound to pass away,
Abandoning my dear boy
   Who is still only so little—
      How will he be able to pass the years?"
When rich man Zhang
   Heard these words,
      He felt as if smothered by knives;
When the mother saw
   Her own darling son,
      Ten thousand swords pierced her heart.
"Because of you
   Your own mother
      Is now being forced to give up the ghost.
Gone to the realm of shade,
   Come to the offices in the earth,
      When will I be able to return to life?

I pray the gods above
    Now I pass away
        To please spare my son, let him live,
And when he thinks of his mother
    Let him burn some paper money[38]
        So his mother may gain a better rebirth."
As woman Yang wept,
    She instructed her husband
        To make arrangements for her funeral,
"And on no account
    Should you ever
        Marry again, have a second wedding.
When a matchmaker
    Comes and talks to you,
        Don't engage in any conversation:
If you marry
    An evil person,
        She will ruin the family, causing death.
And if she would
    Beat you and curse you,
        You would have to suffer in silence.
I pray you, my husband,
    Please show some mercy—
        For better or worse, please do as I say."

Once she had spoken to him,
She didn't dare stay any more,
And was hauled away from her home.
On the road to the underworld
The deepest darkness reigned.
Eventually they came there to
The City of the Unjust Deaths.
The underworld's bitter pain:
You never see any of your relatives.

        While woman Yang was in the underworld
            Her tears fell down without end at the thought

---

38. Sacrificial bank notes made of paper. On the use of paper money in Chinese religion, see Hou 1975 and Scott 2007.

That mother and son would never be reunited
Until she would be released to go back home.

VIII. The Vexations of Her Ladyship Woman Yang in the Underworld

[Shanpoyang]

Woman Yang was in the underworld awash in tears,
"I long for my darling boy,
And I also have no idea which year I'll be able to leave."
Vexation upon vexation,
She could not stop her disconsolate tears.
Her pained weeping was unbearable,
Throughout the year she was unable to stop.
"When will I be able to escape?
Allow me to return to the world of light
So mother and son will be reunited
And I will thank Heaven and Earth.
If I can only see my darling son,
Life and death will be equal to me.
I weep and cry, restless and vexed,
I long for my son but how can he know?
Overcome by grief, restless and vexed—
This longing kills me,
I have no way out."

[Plain prose] Tell that Her Ladyship woman Yang in the underworld as a ghost was embroidering the red gauze and that she could only leave after twelve years.

Tell that the rich man erected a temporary tumulus[39] for his wife in the garden behind his house—but no more about that.

His Lordship the Third Lad personally asked the dragon king of the Eastern Ocean for dragon-beard cloth and a face-fixing pearl to preserve the physical remains of woman Yang—but no more about that.

Now tell that there was a matchmaker woman Kang who on hearing that the rich man had lost his wife came over to propose a match to him.

Woman Kang possessed a sweet tongue and a wily mouth:
"I will make sure to find a match for such a desirable party."

---

39. Literally "a floating tumulus" (fuqiu 浮丘)—a shed to store the coffin at home?

There was a woman Kang,
>   An experienced go-between,
>> Who was eloquent and quite persuasive:
Let her do the talking
>   And of each ten cases
>> Nine would result in a wedding contract.
If there was someone
>   Who was not fitting,
>> She would still call her the very best—
She might harm her parents-in-law
>   And kill the head of the household,
>> Such was her deception and fraud.
This woman Kang
>   Had gathered her things
>> And just had stepped out on the street,
When some other women
>   Who acted as go-betweens
>> Came to her place in order to find her.
They came to speak of
>   That rich man Zhang
>> And his wealth of myriads of strings,[40]
"This is a candidate
>   That if you would speak,
>> He immediately would be persuaded."
When Lady Kang
>   Had but heard one word,
>> She left them hastily and in a hurry:
On her two feet
>   She ran so fast
>> That it seemed as if she were flying.
In just one moment
>   She had arrived
>> Outside the gate of the rich man,
And without asking,
>   Not afraid of the dog,
>> She promptly crashed into the place.

---

40. The common copper coins had a square hole in the middle and were strung on strings of nominally a thousand cash.

When the house boy saw her
And asked her who she was,
Woman Kang did not answer him at all.
She said repeatedly, "Dear boy,
I am as you see a close relative,
Tell the rich man your master
That there is this close relative
Who wants to see him in front."
Repeatedly she called for Master Zhang.

> Woman Kang was an experienced go-between
> But she did not let the rich man know that fact.
> Deliberately she feigned the story she told him,
> Fully confident he was bound to be persuaded.

IX. Woman Kang Visits the Rich Man as Matchmaker

[Shanpoyang]
Now rich man Zhang
Remembered his wife
And silently heaved a sad sigh,
"We have a dear boy
Who is still so young,
But there's none to look after him.
How deeply sad, so deeply sad!
So each day again I'm bound to wonder,
When will you be sent back to the earth?
Only that would fulfill my greatest wish!
Day and night I further continue to think,
Such a fine couple was cruelly separated!
Our only chance to meet
Is in some insubstantial dream.
The household chores are a mess,
Who can take care of them for me?
When will you be allowed to return?
Blue Heaven,
On which day can we be reunited?"

[Plain prose] Now tell that when woman Kang had entered the house, she on purpose asked rich man Zhang, "How long has it been since Her Ladyship woman Yang passed away?" The rich man told her, "Half a year." Woman Kang said, "I regularly see that when you, My Lordship, go out to collect loans, there's something fishy going on around the house. One time I saw in the backyard a man who was carrying a load on his back and leaving on a long trip. Yet another time after you had gone out through the front gate, I saw people carrying five bushels of grain leaving in a great hurry." When the rich man heard this, he was quite annoyed.

>Remembering woman Yang he was heart-broken:
>"Abandoned are father and son here in this house!"

Now rich man Zhang
    Remembering woman Yang,
        Was disconsolate, at a loss what to do;
He pulled over
    His dear little boy
        While tears coursed down his cheeks.
"Now you have died,
    There's none to look after
        The family wealth that is dissipating;
After two or three years
    No hope will be left,
        And we'll end with nothing in our hands.
In the underworld,
    For better or worse,
        You won't be able to hear or to know;
We father and son
    Long for you in vain,
        As no kind of news is communicated.
I long for you,
    You long for me,
        But when will we ever be able to meet?
You long for your son,
    And he longs for you,
        But there is no way to get together.
For the sake of your son
    You in the underworld
        Suffer no end of most bitter misery,

While father and son,
    Here on this earth,
        Have no way to learn information.
During all twelve hours[41]
    There is not a single one
        In which I can set my worries aside,
And at midnight
    I long for you in my dreams,
        Weeping till dawn brightens the sky.
When I then wake up
    And embrace our son,
        My heart is smothered by knives—
In some earlier life
    We failed in our virtue,
        So husband and wife were torn apart.
Your son longs for you
    And involuntarily
        His heart is hurt by a most cruel pain;
We father and son
    Have no way out,
        So our tears flow down in a stream."

When father and son were done weeping,
They, heart-broken, heaved heavy sighs,
Their eyes were awash in tears that were overflowing.
There was no one to look after them,
"Expenses in front emptied the back."[42]
For the sake of her son the mother
Had fallen into the realm of shade.
That they all couldn't live together
Was due to earlier existences through many kalpas.

        When father and son had finished weeping,
           Very soon the dark dusk was falling again.
        Day and night he was longing for his mother:
        Which day would they be able to meet again?

---

41. In traditional China the full day was divided into twelve hours, not twenty-four.
42. This line probably means that in the absence of a capable housekeeper the expenditures the family has to make quickly will exhaust its reserves.

X. Little Huaxian Longs for His Mother

[Weeping through the Five Watches][43]

In the night's first watch
I am o so lonely and sad,
As I think of my mother my tears course down.
When will she have finished embroidering and be released?
Only then will mother and son be reunited.
O my dear Buddha,
Only then will mother and son be reunited.

In the night's second watch
I weep and I holler and cry.
As I think of my mother I cannot catch any sleep.
Two or three times in a row I call, "Dear mother,
Why did you abandon me with no place to go?
O my dear Buddha,
Why did you abandon me with no place to go?"

In the night's third watch
I cannot support the pain,
As sleeping I long for my mother in my dream.
When will they allow you to come back home?
If I could see your face, I'd be filled with hope.
O my dear Buddha,
If I could see your face, I'd be filled with hope.

In the night's fourth watch
My tears still will not dry.
Because of your son you are in the underworld.
When will you finish your embroidery and return?
Only then can mother and son meet once again.
O my dear Buddha,
Only then can mother and son meet once again.

In the night's fifth watch,
The sky slowly turns bright.

---

43. In traditional China the night was divided into five watches. Songs made up of five stanzas lamenting one's fate have a tradition that goes back at least to the ninth and tenth centuries.

The golden rooster announces dawn, the jade hare sinks.
My dear mother, when will you leave your dark abode?
This longing kills me—we never receive any news.
O my dear Buddha,
This longing kills me—we never receive any news.

[Plain prose] Tell that the little boy Huaxian was longing for his mother and wept all night—but no more about that.

Now tell that woman Kang came once again to propose a match. When she had greeted the rich man, she only talked about some gossip and deliberately didn't raise the subject. But after tea had been served, woman Kang said, "Woman Yang will only be able to return after she has spent twelve years in the underworld embroidering her red gauze. If the underworld authorities release her, then all is fine, but what to do if they don't release her? Sir, you spend a lot of time on the road and are rarely at home, so I am afraid that your family affairs may suffer." When the rich man heard this, he asked, "What would then be the best?" Woman Kang said, "I only fear I can't find a good one, so let me make a careful search."

> Woman Kang had a glib mouth and a capable tongue,
> For better or worse she was set to arrange this match.

Tell that woman Kang
    Had taken her leave
        And returned to her own house,
But she didn't go home
    But went straightaway
        To "hairpins and skirt" woman You.
She entered her room
    And greeted the woman,
        Then sat down to propose the match,
"I come here today
    To propose to you
        A marriage with an excellent party."
When this woman You
    Had eagerly heard this,
        She was secretly pleased in her heart,
"If you bring this about,
    I'll reward you handsomely,
        To thank you for this great service.

If you mention me,
   I am only afraid
      That that rich man will not take me."
"Once you have married
   That rich man Zhang,
      You'll forever enjoy status and wealth."
So woman You said,
   "Dear aunt Kang,
      Please give it all your best efforts.
When the deal is done,
   I'll reward you richly
      To thank you for this great service."
Now old dame Kang
   Said to woman You,
      "I don't dare make you any promises.
Since ancient times
   Haven't there also been
      People who go back on a marriage?"

When woman Kang had spoken,
Woman You was fully informed:
This deal would definitely be arranged.
Woman Kang knew how to talk
And could move people's hearts.
Both sides were quite pleased,
The business was fairly settled.
Poor and rich were not equal,
But for better or worse, the deal was struck.

      Woman Kang was a persuasive talker,
      And woman You was an evil bedmate.
      The golden lad was to suffer murder
      And experience torment and torture.

XI. Woman You Marries Rich Man Zhang

[Shanpoyang]
Rich man Zhang
Had been fated
To lose his wife through death.

It was too because the left golden lad would meet with misfortune.
By marrying the evil-hearted woman You
The star of destruction made its appearance.
It was also because Her Ladyship woman Yang suffered her karmic fate:
She embroidered red gauze in the underworld for twelve long years.
Mother and son were separated
And both of them suffered torture and deceit.
What bitter pain, vexation, and trouble!
Ah,
When, alas, will woman Yang return?
For the sake of her little boy
She fell into the underworld.

[Plain prose] Tell that woman Kang after two or three visits had talked rich man Zhang around. So he conducted the engagement ceremony with woman You, and after choosing a lucky hour and an auspicious day he took woman You into his house as his wife.

Now tell that after he had married woman You for more than a year, he engaged in business to support his family. The little boy Huaxian stayed with woman You, who also had a son of her own. This boy was nine years old and the little boy Huaxian six years, and the two of them were always fighting.

> Woman You, evil and mean, was not fair-minded:
> All through the day she was abusing the little boy.

Woman You thought,
   "Little boy Huaxian,
      You truly, truly are detestable!
Time and again
   You throw a tantrum
      And don't listen to what I say.
When I today
   Call you over
      To listen to maternal advice,
You curse me out
   As an evil stepmother,
      Infuriating my motherly heart!"
When rich man Zhang
   As it happened one day
      Had left home to collect loans,

Woman You called
   For that damned bastard,
      Wanting to give him a beating.
Lifting the cudgel
   She gave him some strokes,
      But he did not show any fear,
So she gathered thorns
   And threw a handful,
      Threw them all over his body.
She beat him a while,
   Then hauled him a while:
      Broken skin and gaping wounds!
The broken thorns
   Stuck in his flesh;
      His body was covered in blood.
When he wanted to weep,
   He didn't dare weep,
      Afraid he'd get yet another beating;
When he wanted to cry,
   He didn't dare cry,
      Suppressing his rage, choking his voice.
The gates in front and in back
   Had both been tightly closed,
      And as she beat him she asked him,
"For half a year
   You have never
      Called me 'mother' even once!
You'll not be able
   To escape with your life,
      You will die here at my hands,
Because if I don't
   Beat you to death,
      I'll never be reborn as a human.
I'll torture you,
   This karmic enemy,
      Until you'll have lost your life,
And rich man Zhang
   For all his money
      Won't have the gall to kill me!"

And she cried out,
  "You little scoundrel,
    Listen to your mother's order:
When your old man
  Asks you about it,
    Say that you suffered a headache."

When she had beaten the child,
The rich man came back home.
When he saw the boy, he was awash in tears.
Time and again he called out,
"Tell me, my dear little boy,
Who gave you this beating?
I'll never forgive that person."
When he took off his clothes,
He saw his whole body was covered in blood.

> The rich man was deeply grieved
> And beat up that no-good woman.
> "How do you dare abuse my son?
> Vent your anger on your bastard!"

XII. Rich Man Zhang Gives Woman You, His Evil Wife, a Beating

[Miandaxu]
When the rich man saw his son,
He felt his heart was ripped out,
And cried, "My dear little child,
This is all because of your father's fault!"
Deeply pained in his heart,
He bitterly wept, moved by pain.
"I didn't listen to woman Yang,
And now this indeed has occurred!
My dear son, now you had to suffer—
When will your own mother leave the realm of shade?"

[Plain prose] When rich man Zhang entered the gate and saw his son, his tears welled up as a spring. He paid no attention to woman You's explanation, but grabbed her by her black hair and gave her a beating. Holding the child in his arms, he saw when he looked more carefully that thorns were hooked in his flesh over his whole body, so that whenever he stroked the child, it cried from pain.

> The father held his darling little son in his arms;
> As tears flowed from his eyes, he wailed loudly.

He gave a cry,
  "My little son,
    Through what kind of evil karma
Did I have to see
  That that no-good wife
    Is cruelly killing my dear little boy?
All over your body
  Are fragments of thorns,
    So your skin and flesh are inflamed,
I will have someone
  Pull them all out
    Without drenching you in the pus."
Little Huaxian
  Cried out, "Dear father,
    Please do not touch or disturb them,
As soon as you move
  A single one I die—
    The pain is killing your little boy."
He cried out once,
  "My dear mother,
    Where did you go, where are you?
You gave birth to me,
  But when barely six,
    We mother and son were separated.
Because of your son,
  You, my dear mother,
    Were taken down to the underworld;
By the looks of it,
  I will be killed by abuse
    And leave to meet with King Yama.
When you think of me,
  You have no idea
    How this stepmother mistreats me,

But I know that you
   Now live in the underworld
      Only for the sake of your little boy.
You must suffer
   There for twelve years,
      And your son has to suffer his fate,
But if mother and son
   Could meet only once,
      I would die without any regret.
But then I'm afraid
   That my stepmother
      Will abuse me so much I will die,
And when you come out,
   You will not find me—
      All suffering will have been in vain."

When father and son stopped weeping,
They, heart-broken, heaved heavy sighs.
Woman You was filled with a towering rage.
In her heart she secretly considered
How she might kill that little child.
Once the rich man would be away,
She would commit that cruel deed.
"All loose bones in a bubbling wok,
Even that isn't enough to please my heart!"

      Woman You had decided on the deed:
      She wanted to do away with the child.
      "When the rich man is out of the house,
      I will make sure that you cannot live."

XIII. Woman You Heats the Wok to Harm the Little Boy

[Shanpoyang]
Little Huaxian's
Eyes were filled with disconsolate tears.
He held on to his father crying again and again,
"Please, don't go away!
My stepmother will beat me,

Her cruel heart has no feeling at all!
When she beats me to death,
Where can I go hide myself?
But if you refuse to stay at home
And definitely have to collect those loans,
Not listening to your son's words,
I will not dare loudly weep,
But silently drop my tears,
Filled with sadness.
When you abandon me here,
I will suffer vicious torments,
Filled with sadness.
And if she beats me to death,
Your remorse comes too late."

[Plain prose] Tell that the rich man instructed little Huaxian, "My son, tomorrow I have to collect those loans. You stay at home and don't go outdoors." Little Huaxian grabbed his father's clothes and said, "Daddy, don't go! When you go, my mother will beat me again!" The rich man said, "Don't worry! She would not dare give you another beating." Having said that, he got on his horse and left. When woman You saw that he had left, she immediately conceived a vicious plan. She heated a wok of boiling water and placed her little enemy inside the wok. "Only when he is cooked to a pulp will I be pleased."

>One wok of boiling water, seething and roaring:
>She grabbed her enemy and committed the deed.

Tell that woman You
    Fooled Huaxian
        And tightly grabbed the little boy,
She squeezed his arms,
    Lifted him by his feet,
        And so robbed him of his true soul.
Thousand-Mile Eye
    Reported this in a hurry
        To His Lordship the Third Lad:
"That woman You
    Had killed the boy
        In a boiling, roiling, seething wok!"

When the Third Lad
    Had heard this tale,
        He immediately arrived on the spot
And saw woman You
    Lift up the little boy
        And then throw him into the wok.
The divine Third Lad
    Manifested his powers
        And his divine hand stopped her,
But on one hand [of the boy],
    Touched by the boiling water,
        One layer of skin had shriveled.
Now woman You
    Was flurried and flustered,
        Afraid someone might see her,
So she hurriedly
    Rinsed some beans
        And put those in that wok,
While the little boy,
    Suffering his pain,
        Was shaking all over his body—
He wanted to weep,
    But feared to be beaten
        (His gall shaking,[44] his heart scared),
And thought to himself,
    "My dear mother,
        How can you know what happens?
Your darling son
    Was thrown in a wok,
        To remove the grass with its roots.
The first time around
    She beat me with thorns
        From top to toe all over my body;
This time around
    She killed your son
        In a boiling, roiling, seething wok.
When father left,
    I tried repeatedly
        To make him stay but failed to do so;

---

44. The gall is the seat of courage.

Only thinking about cash
   He doesn't think about you
      And your offspring, your little boy.
If my stepmother
   Tries once more
      To harm and kill your darling son,
The family wealth
   Will completely
      Fall into the hands of my stepmother.
Now at present
   She beats and curses
      Your darling son completely at will,
Not fearing Heaven,
   Not fearing Earth,
      She is out to murder your little son."
When little Huaxian
   Had stopped weeping,
      His father had arrived on the scene,
And seeing his son
   Had scalded his hand,
      He repeatedly called out his grief.
He asked woman You,
   "How come our son
      Has managed to scald his hand?"
Holding his son
   He felt smothered by knives—
      Ten thousand swords pierced his heart!
He called out,
   "My dear little son,
      The pain is killing your dear father!
How can your mother
   Down in the underworld
      Manage to learn about these things?"

The rich man most bitterly wept
And repeatedly wanted to know,
"How could he burn one layer of skin?"
Woman You replied in this way,
"My husband, please understand.
There was this one wok of beans

And the boy wanted to eat some.
Wanting to dredge some up,
He scalded his hand, burning his skin."

> Woman You was a glib-tongued harpy
> But barely succeeded in covering this up.
> "If that little bastard wants to accuse me,
> He will only get himself a good lesson."

XIV. The Rich Man Comes Home and Woman You Covers Things Up

[Yifengshu]
How could the rich man bear the pain?
That marriage had not lasted that long,
When they had been cruelly separated.
In the underworld she must be weeping
And their son could not see his mother—
She longs for her son, he for his mother.
Disconsolate by pain,
Overcome by sadness.
How can he stand his stepmother's abuse?
Come to think of it, it is quite hard:
People's life in this world is not perfect.
You have no children or you have no cash:
It clearly is all settled by your former life.
Don't blame Heaven for poverty or lack of children.
When you ask for the root,
If your wealth is complete,
Husband and wife and children will not be complete.

[Plain prose] Tell that when the rich man and his son had wept, he again considered that there were many accounts outside that all were due by the end of this month, so he said to his son, "If I don't go now, it will be impossible to collect them later." When the little boy heard this, tears sprang from his eyes, and he held tightly onto his father's clothes, not releasing him for the life of it. This very much pained the rich man, who despite all objections really didn't want to leave. But it concerned quite a lot of money, so he could only send the boy with some lie to his room, go outside, get on his horse, and leave. Once woman You had seen the rich man leave, her mind was occupied with the thought how best to do away with the little boy.

> Woman You was quite agitated in her heart:
> With poison she killed this thorn in her eye.

Tell that woman You
   Went personally
      To buy a package of poison;
In the drug store
   She asked the physician
      But he refused to comply.
But woman You said,
   "It isn't for nothing,"
      And offered ten ounces of silver;
When the physician saw
   That snow-white silver,
      Cupidity changed his mind.
"I will give her
   This package of poison
      In some other, secluded place—
If someone is poisoned,
   No one has seen me,
      So they cannot trace it to me."
When woman You
   Had received the poison,
      She took it back home with her,
And once in her room
   She used the poison
      To do away with the little boy.
One bowl of pork
   And one bowl of rice,
      Both mixed with the poison:
As soon as the child,
   Had eaten that down,
      He encountered King Yama!
His whole body
   Had turned black;
      Flames emerged from his mouth.
The little child
   Struggled for his life
      While smoke rose up from his belly.

The Third Lad
   In his temple
      Soon learned this state of affairs
And took one miracle pill
   And one bowl of water
      That he infused in his stomach.
He lifted the child,
   He lifted it up,
      And then placed it in water:
Soaked for a while
   He was saved at last—
      Only then his soul returned.
When little Huaxian
   Woke up again,
      He spat out a bloody fluid,
But he could not speak
   And could not talk,
      As he was sunk in a haze.
For two or three days
   He didn't want to take
      Brown soup or cold water:
The left golden lad
   Had been murdered
      And survived but by a hair.

Woman You thought to herself,
"This attempt did not work out.
Several times my attempts have failed,
One way or another he didn't die,
As before he comes back to life.
After these two or three attempts,
I am really pissed off about this:
Let me get a knife of finest steel
And murder that boy once and for all!"

      Woman You was bereft of any feeling,
      She did the boy in by the use of poison.
      Inside her mind she secretly hid a knife,
      Always intent on murdering someone.

XV. Woman You Does in Little Boy Huaxian Using Poison

[Pangzhuangtai]
It's quite incomprehensible:
All my attempts so far didn't succeed.
When I killed him in boiling water, he failed to die,
And when I did him in with poison, he also revived.
Every time I tried to murder that little bastard,
That archfiend was never harmed one little bit.
O how I hate the fact
That I didn't succeed:
For better or worse I'll kill that little boy!

[Plain prose] Tell that woman You had used poison to do little Huaxian in but that he did not die. She instructed old and young in the household, all the servants employed by the family, not to say a word about the fact that little Huaxian had died from poisoning, "Of course there will be a handsome reward for you!" But no more about this incident.

Now tell that rich man Zhang had used all the money he had collected to acquire the office of commandant. He was stationed at Jiujiang, where he made camp and built fortifications. Who could have known that the pirate Liu Hong would rebel and lead all his troops to plunder Jiujiang—he killed three thousand government troops, not leaving a single one. The rich man was thrown into the capital prison and condemned to death.[45]

> On hearing her husband was condemned to die,
> The stepmother set out to murder the little boy.

When woman You
    Heard the news
        Her husband was condemned to death,
She was filled with joy
    And laid her plans
        For his wealth and for the little boy.
Woman You ordered
    The blacksmith to make
        A knife made of the finest steel,

---

45. As commander, rich man Zhang is held responsible for the defeat of the government troops.

"Once I have killed
　　That little archfiend,
　　　　I will be able to live a decent life."
Now woman You
　　Had a son of her own
　　　　That was nine years old at the time,
While little Huaxian
　　Was barely six years of age
　　　　And living apart from his mother.
This woman You
　　Said, "This night
　　　　That little bastard, little Huaxian,
That little archfiend
　　Is bound to die,
　　　　Is set to meet with King Yama!
My own boy,
　　My dear son,
　　　　I will lay down against the wall,
And little Huaxian
　　Will be laid down
　　　　In the front when going to bed."
This woman You,
　　Hiding her knife,
　　　　Had made up her mind to strike,
But the Third Lad
　　With his divine eye
　　　　Also already had been informed.
He entered the room
　　And placed the little one
　　　　On the inside against the wall,
And placed the big one
　　Now outside in front,
　　　　Without anyone knowing a thing.
Tell that woman You
　　Sharpened her knife
　　　　And all night never closed an eye,
Waiting for the third watch
　　To commit the dire deed
　　　　And kill and murder the little boy.

She rushed into the room
    Which was so pitch dark
        She could not tell little from big:
She felt for a head
    And with one slash
        The blood was spurting all over.
When she took the head
    She still did not know
        That she had killed her own son;
Only when she lit a lamp
    Did she see the truth—
        Stamping her feet, beating her breast,
She cried out,
    "My dear son,
        Your mother was blind in both eyes!
I did not suspect
    You might change places
        And were sleeping at the outside.
With eyes wide-open
    I mistakenly killed
        My own child, my dear darling son!
The pain kills your mom,
    My plans were in vain,
        I did not succeed in my aim.
When I see my son,
    The corpse and the head,
        I feel as if my lungs are gouged.
I killed my son by mistake
    And I feel such pain as if
        Ten thousand swords pierce my heart.
Had I known this before
    I would outside the room
        Have lit a lamp to give me some light!
Involuntarily
    I am filled with fear,
        My gall shaking, my heart so scared.
What kind of affair!
    How dare I shout?
        Other people might learn the facts!

> I'll steel myself
>> And will only say
>>> The little boy killed his big brother."

She called the whole household together,
All those many male servants and maids,
So everyone should come and see this for himself
How the little one had had the courage
To commit the foul deed of fratricide—
"If he is capable of killing his brother,
He'll also want to murder his mother.
If I don't take the cursed boy to court,
Even I as mother may be charged with the crime!"

> "I will go and lodge a formal accusation,
> When doing things, it must be done right.
> Now he has killed my dear little darling,
> None of us can harbor any hope at all!"

XVI. After Woman You Has Mistakenly Killed Her Son, She Lodges an Accusation

[Shanpoyang]
Now this woman You
Had a venomous heart
And committed outrageous acts.
Killing her own son by mistake
She had absolutely no evidence,
But overcome by great sadness
Went to court and lodged an accusation.
Steeling her bloody heart,
She bribed the clear judge,
Giving him a hundred taels.[46]
But of course Heaven knows the facts.
Torture will result in a confession,
A confession that allows no pardon.
"Torture results in a confession:

---

46. One tael is one ounce of silver.

Once in prison I won't send any food
So that little imp will starve to death."

[Plain prose] When woman You had killed her own son by mistake, her grief was unbearable, and she went to court to lodge an accusation. Hauling the little boy along, she knelt down in front of the court hall. When the magistrate ascended the hall and received the accusation, he asked woman You after reading it, "A little kid of six that kills the older one of nine? This case makes no sense, there must be some deception."

Now tell that a flustered woman You came forward on her knees, and took one hundred ounces of white silver from her purse, "Your Excellency, this is only a first gift. Each year at each of the four seasons I will present you with a hundred ounces without any exception." The district magistrate then shouted, "Woman, move back. Bring the little one forward!" He interrogated him, "Was it you who killed your elder brother? If you quickly confess you will be spared a beating. Better own up to it." The little one was afraid of a beating and owned up to the murder. "Truly deserving the death sentence," he signed his confession and was taken to prison.

> The little kid was so scared he confessed under duress;
> Having signed the confession, he was taken to prison.

The court clerk said,
  "Little Huaxian,
    I've taken down your confession.
Once you have signed,
  We'll take you to prison
    Where you'll be locked in a cell.
We'll wait till autumn,
  After the autumn assizes,[47]
    And then you too will be killed."
This little boy
  Kept on crying,
    And wailed at the top of his voice.
Inside his cell
  It was totally black,
    He couldn't see the sun in the sky.
He had no relatives,
  He had no old friends,
    And was bound to die of starvation.

---

47. Death sentences that had been pronounced locally by the magistrate were submitted to the central government for review and could be executed only once they had been confirmed by the emperor.

He loudly called,
   "My dear mother,
      How can you know what happened?
And my own father—
   Where may he be?
      We never received any news.
Does he live?
   Has he died?
      His circumstances are unclear,
And the many millions
   Have all ended up
      In my stepmother's possession.
Both father and son
   As well as my mother—
      What karma is this from a former life?
We are all separated
   In three different places
      And cannot enjoy a moment of ease!
There's no way out,
   And I have no idea
      Of the bitter vexations of each of them.
This is the evil karma
   Of five hundred kalpas
      Of former existences coming home!
My father in prison,
   His son in this cell,
      My mother down in the underworld:
This pains me to death
   And without any help
      I am bound to lose here my life.
When you are wealthy
   Or have many relatives,
      There are ways around the law;
My bitter death
   Only Heaven will know,
      But without eyes still it's blind.
In this prison,
   Here in my cell,
      I clearly suffer my punishment;

Both day and night
    Torture is applied
        So I never will have any rest.
When evening comes,
    I am tied to my bed
        So I cannot move hands or feet,
And across my body
    They throw a belly rope
        So I cannot turn my body around.
I'm stuck by lice,
    I'm bitten by fleas,
        And I am sucked dry by bedbugs;
Then there are rats
    That are as big as cats
        And come and chew on my heels.
If you have relatives
    Who bring you food,
        You're half hungry, half filled,
But without relatives
    It is bitter vexations
        As your child starves to death."

When Huaxian had finished weeping,
He suddenly heard the announcement
And all the people in prison knew very well
That the frost-like verdict had arrived,
The sentence of death for the inmates!
Disconsolate, overcome by vexation;
Bitterly weeping and wounded inside:
He had signed to the truth of the facts,
The final decision allowed for no pardon!

        The three courts had signed the papers:
        Those banished left to serve as troops.
        Strangulation? You got one degree less.
        But beheading? You were not spared.[48]

---

48. Imprisonment was not used as a punishment. Criminals might be condemned to banishment, and this might be combined with a condemnation to serve in the army as a common soldier. Strangulation, which left the corpse complete, was considered a lighter punishment than beheading and given for

XVII. After the Autumn Assizes Little Huaxian Is about to Be Beheaded

[Zhufeiyun]
There's no escape from one's karma:
A little boy of seven years will be executed!
If His Lordship will not learn about this,
His fate, whether life or death, is unknown.
"My Buddha,
I'm clearly wrongly killed!
I pray the Three Offices
To record this very clearly,
So revenge can be exacted!"

[Plain prose] Now tell that when little Huaxian had wept for quite a while, the criminals were all taken to the execution ground. His Lordship the Third Lad also had learned about this in time, and in a moment he had arrived at the execution ground, where he had a huge whirlwind lift up little Huaxian and gently put him down in the abandoned wilds outside the city. His Lordship the Third Lad rose into the air and loudly proclaimed, "My child, don't go back home. Go directly to the Eastern Capital to find your father there in the southern prison."[49]

When the divine manifestation had disappeared, little Huaxian was overcome by vexation, and without a clear sense of direction he went where his feet would lead him, weeping and crying without end. He happened to run into an old man who, when he saw Huaxian, asked what had happened. Huaxian told him the whole story from beginning to end. That old man said, "My child, you are quite pitiable. I will give you three hundred copper coins as traveling money to go to the capital and find your father." When Huaxian thanked him with a bow, that old man turned into a gust of fresh air and disappeared.

While on the road the little boy was quite disconsolate:
"Will I ever be able to see my dear mother once again?"

Little Huaxian
  Went his lonely way
    Through the wild fields outside town;

---

lighter offenses. Beheading was seen as a more severe punishment because the body was separated from the head. The crimes that deserved beheading were more serious and would be less easily pardoned.

49. The Eastern Capital in vernacular literature usually refers to Kaifeng, the capital of the Northern Song dynasty. As the story is set in the Tang dynasty, it here must refer to the capital Chang'an (modern Xi'an). The southern prison is the metropolitan prison, in contrast to the palace prison.

He had no relatives,
    He had no good friends,
        So where would he be able to rest?
As he walked a mile,
    He wept for a mile,
        His stomach feeling the pangs of hunger;
Tea nor rice
    Could he buy anywhere,
        So the little boy was starving to death.
So he cried out,
    "Dear father and mother,
        You are not taking care of your child!
Now rich man Zhang's
    Son is begging for food,
        Leaving behind a foul reputation.
Because of my hunger
    I cannot walk further,
        My limbs are without any force;
When evening comes,
    The inns where I stay
        Are only the abandoned tile kilns.
Because of her son
    My dear mother
        Evidently is suffering punishment:
I have caused my mother
    To be implicated to such a degree
        That she is not even sure of her life.
My dear father
    Has in the court of justice
        Been condemned to the death penalty,
But I, this child,
    Have had the luck
        To escape from death with my life.
If I succeed
    In finding my father,
        Father and son will be reunited;
If we can get together,
    We clearly will be
        People who enjoy a second life!

But if something
> Untoward happens
>> To my father there in that prison,
He'll abandon his son
> Without any refuge
>> So he'll be a beggar for all his life.
We, father and son—
> I have no clue because
>> Of which karma from which life—
Have been dispersed
> Over three places
>> Without ever finding any rest.
If father survives
> And mother will live
>> And father and son are reunited,
Then your pitiable son
> Will have endured
>> A thousand escapes from certain death!"

Walking on, little Huaxian
Had for some days on end
Not dared spend a night at an inn,
Resting by the roadside
Only in dilapidated kilns.
Could he stay, he stayed.
Slowly making headway
He asked people he met
How best to find his father in prison.

> The little child in an abandoned kiln
> Wrecked by emotion cried and wept.
> Longing at night for dad and mom,
> He saw them a few times in a dream.

XVIII. In an Abandoned Kiln Little Huaxian Longs for His Father and Mother

[Weeping through the five watches]

In the night's first watch,
I feel oh so lonely and sad.

At night I seek shelter in an abandoned kiln,
The hunger is insupportable, I cannot sleep.
With wide open eyes I suffer most cruelly.
O my dear Buddha,
With wide open eyes I suffer most cruelly.

In the night's second watch
I weep and I cry and I wail.
Longing for my dear mother, I cannot sleep.
The family wealth of millions isn't managed,
Mother and son are dispersed with no refuge.
O my dear Buddha,
Mother and son are dispersed with no refuge.

In the night's third watch
I long for my dear mom.
Alone and lonely I shed a thousand tears.
If my mother would be robbed of her life,
It would kill me to be without any hope.
O my dear Buddha,
It would kill me to be without any hope.

In the night's fourth watch,
My tears resemble a spring.
For my sake my mother dwells in the underworld.
Father and mother and child are not united together:
When will we ever be able to see each other again?
O my dear Buddha,
When will we ever be able to see each other again?

In the night's fifth watch
The Jade Hare[50] urges me
To ask for precise information at break of dawn.
After asking the innkeeper for true specifications
I gather the courage to make my way to his cell.
O my dear Buddha,
I gather the courage to go and visit my father.

---

50. The Jade Hare inhabits the moon.

[Plain prose] Tell that little Huaxian came to visit his father—but no more about it.

After rich man Zhang had lost his troops as well as his officers and hurt the common people, the imperial court had him arrested and placed in the southern prison. There was no one to bring him any food.[51] He had sent letters home, but had received no reply, and suffered no end of hunger and cold. "This was all my own mistake. First of all, I should never have married a second wife, and secondly I should not have acquired this office of commandant. Here I suffer misery, and I have no clue about the situation at home. I'm afraid the child is bound to suffer abuse at the hands of woman You, and I don't know when woman Yang will return from the underworld. I've brought about the ruin of my family and the death of its members. But now remorse is too late!"

> Thinking about family affairs, knives cut up his lungs;
> Longing for his wife and son, swords pierce his heart.

The rich man wept
    As there in prison
        He was disconsolate, filled with vexations,
"My whole family
    Has died bitterly,
        Without any hope for a better rebirth.
Even if woman Yang
    Would come back to life,
        Her corpse and head would be decomposed.
As for the little boy,
    I have no clue
        Whether he has died or is still alive.
Those millions in cash
    Will have been wasted
        By that second wife, woman You;
And who did take care
    Of all the family possessions—
        On whom could I there rely?
Now if woman Yang
    Would still be alive,
        Who would dare even touch them?

---

51. Prisons provided no food, so prisoners depended for their survival on food provided by relatives and friends.

If one but has
   An adult son or daughter,
      One doesn't have to fear anyone.
But now I suffer
   Cold and hunger,
      Far too much to support for a moment.
Why not go begging?
   Locked in my cell
      I am not allowed to go out of the gate.
Of all people in the world
   There is no one who is
      As bitterly vexed as our household:
The three of us
   Must in an earlier life
      Have murdered, massacred people!
It must be because
   When loaning out money,
      The main sum was little, the interest high,
So those poor devils
   Must have hated my guts,
      Causing damage to sons and grandsons.
I pray Blue Heaven:
   If my poor little son
      And my dear wife would still be alive,
I would be happy
   Even if I for the rest of my life
      Had to go begging from door to door."
As rich man Zhang
   Was vexed by worries,
      The warden came in and reported,
"There is this
   Little kid
      That has come to the prison,
And he says that
   Rich man Zhang
      Is the father who sired him.
In his hand he carries
   A broken wooden bowl
      And his eyes are awash in tears."

When rich man Zhang
   Had heard these words,
      He hastily went over to have a look,
And for sure it was
   Really his own son,
      That little boy, his dear darling.
He opened the gate
   To let him inside.
      The boy threw his arms around him,
At which his father
   Was overcome by shock
      And fell down on the dusty floor.
Little Huaxian
   Cried repeatedly,
      "Dear father, come back to life!"
All other criminals
   There in the prison
      Seeing this were moved to sighs.
The little boy
   Wept quite some time
      Before this father had revived
And held his son
   In his embrace,
      Wailing at the top of his voice.

Father and son were reunited:
People who had a second life!
The father questioned his little boy
How he begged for his food,
And how he had left his home?
So he heard him tell the story:
He had barely escaped death,
And only after many dangers
Had he been able to sneak away.

      The father remained in his cell
      As the boy left the prison again.
      "Because that god has saved me,
      I escaped from death still alive."

XIX. Little Huaxian Visits the Prison and Father and Son Are Reunited

[Shanpoyang]
When little Huaxian
Came to the prison,
He there saw his dad,
And he loudly repeatedly cried,
"We father and son
Must in some earlier life
Have created the karma
That threatens our lives,
But only Heaven will know."
They wept unbearably:
Father and son saw no way out.
The wife in the underworld—
Alive or dead, who could tell?
There's no escape from karma,
That's why they suffered this misery;
There's no escape from karma,
That's why they suffered this misery.

[Plain prose] Little Huaxian had arrived at the prison and found his father. They wept for a while, and told their whole stories from the beginning. The son asked his father, "Have you had some food?" "From where should I have had some food these last few days?" So little Huaxian said, "Let me go out and beg some food for you." Beating out "Lotus Flowers Fall" he went begging.[52]

When lotus flowers arise, they come from the mouth of a hare;
When lotus flowers fall, they enter into the guts of a chicken;[53]
And when lotus flowers turn, they permeate the ten directions.
  Borrowing these flowers, they brightly show the Dharma King.[54]
Pervading mountains and oceans He knows no hindrance at all;
Proceeding from east to west He shines with a brilliant radiance.
  The agonized little boy was extremely disconsolate and scared
And on the main street he piteously implored men and women,

---

52. "Lotus Flowers Fall" is the typical begging song.
53. The hare (or rabbit) stands for the hour *mao* (5–7 A.M.); the chicken (rooster) stands for the hour *you* (5–7 P.M.).
54. The Dharma King (the Buddha) is often depicted seated on a lotus flower.

"Don't throw away any leftover tea or any superfluous food,
But give it to me, this poor little boy who met with misfortune.
   My dear father has been locked up in the prefectural prison
And all day long never sees any rice or any other sustenance.
Starving from hunger my dear father is about to pass away:
If you will save my parents, we will never forget your grace."

   After each word that he called he wept again for quite a while,
It broke the hearts of people who were made of iron or stone.
From both sides of the street people all came over to ask him,
"Little boy, please tell us, to which family do you belong?

   Your looks are quite handsome, your face spells nobility,
Why are you weeping so piteously, tears coursing down?
Where on earth is your home, and where were you born?
Are your father and mother alive and where do they live?

   We're afraid that you may have lost your way back home:
Once we know where that is, we'll happily take you there.
Do you remember the name and surname of your parents?
Is it Zhang? Is it Wang? Is it Li? Is it Zhao? Or any other?"

   "As you kind-hearted men and women ask these questions,
Please listen as I will tell you my feelings from the start.
Since generations our family lived in the village Huaxian;
My mother was surnamed Yang, my father was a Zhang.

   My father is rich man Zhang, well known for his wealth,
And my mother woman Yang was a very capable woman.
Advanced in years my father and mother had no offspring,
So went to the temple of the Third Lad to light incense.

   I was born after they had made a great vow to the deity,
But when I had but turned three, I was struck by disaster:
His Lordship the Third Lad came to claim the past vow,
And took my true soul with him back to his temple hall.

   My dear mother promised to embroider a gauze curtain,
And finishing it in three years hung it up in the temple.
When the other divinities had seen it, they all loved it
And they all praised my mother for her fine embroidery.

   They then came and took away my mother's true soul
And had her as a ghost embroider red gauze down below.
When her work will be finished in another twelve years,
They will allow my mother to return to her own home.

   My aged father believed the glib words of a go-between
And married a woman You, a person without any virtue.

Her heart was only concerned about the son of her own
And repeatedly she tried to rob me, this kid, of my life.
   Now mistakenly killing her own dear son instead of me
She came up with a scheme to repay his life with mine.
At the execution in autumn a mighty whirlwind rose up
By which the deity saved me from the execution ground.
   From the sky he instructed me to go and find my father—
I had no clue that my father had broken the imperial law!
Locked up in prison he is starving and quickly will die,
That's why I am here now begging you for your help.
   I only came begging to save my dear father from death—
Please take pity on this one family that is all dispersed!"
From the beginning he told them all his many sufferings
While from his eyes poured in streams his sad tears.

When these people heard this,
Everyone was deeply moved.
"You are such a handsome little boy,
But your one family suffered,
Now dispersed in three places.
That woman You is no good
With a heart of iron or stone.
She tried to kill you so often
And wrecked your family—how evil!"

> The people were all moved to sighs
> And involuntarily felt disconsolate.
> They donated money and gave food
> Out of pity for the dear little boy.

XX. To the Beat of "Lotus Flowers Fall" Little Huaxian Begs for Food and Saves His Father

[Miandaxu]
Little Huaxian
Clearly met with misfortune,
It was due to a former life
That they couldn't be together,
Couldn't employ the family wealth of millions.
Suffering misfortune

The father and his son
Were separated, apart!
Longing for his mother
He couldn't be reunited.
The mother was in the underworld
Embroidering red gauze—
The end was near!

[Plain prose] Tell that little Huaxian was seeking tea and begging food to the beat of "Lotus Flowers Fall" to filially provide for his father. His sincerity moved old and young along the main street and in the lanes on both sides, so they all donated to him.

Before one had noticed eleven years had passed. Now tell that the Son of Heaven, the King of the Tang, had a daughter, Princess Cuiwei, who had not yet found a consort. At the crossing of a busy market a bunted loft was erected, and all people, whether military or civilian, rich or poor, came there to catch the colored ball: the one to be hit would be the prince consort![55] Little Huaxian also passed below the bunted loft, with his brown earthenware cup in his hands. After the princess had prayed to the empty sky, she threw down her embroidered ball, and it landed nowhere else but in Huaxian's earthenware cup. When the princess saw this, she said, "Too bad! This is fate." Tell that he was promptly invited to enter the palace and change his dress, and after a day had been chosen, the wedding was celebrated.

> Little Huaxian had been begging for food for eleven springs
> But now he'll enjoy glory and prosperity as a prince consort.

Little Huaxian,
   Now in the palace,
      Felt sad at the thought of his father,
"I allow my own father
   To die of starvation—
      I, this child without any filial piety!
And also my dear mother
   Suffers for her son
      No end of torture and tribulation,
While their son today
   As a prince consort
      Has forgotten about both his parents.

---

55. While this is a quite common way for a highborn young lady to choose a husband in traditional vernacular literature, no such custom is attested in other sources.

I may be loyal[56]
    But I am not filial
        Because my father dies of starvation,
The thunder will strike
    This unfilial son,
        This little boy that kills his parents!"
When the princess saw
    The prince consort weeping,
        She stepped forward and asked him,
"What is the cause
    That you today
        Are so deeply moved in your heart?"
The prince consort replied,
    "Princess, please listen:
        My dear father is locked up in prison
Without relative or friend
    Who brings him his food—
        He relies completely on me, his son."
The princess said,
    "How can such a matter
        At present be of any importance at all?
I'll tell my father the king
    To grant him a pardon,
        So he can walk out of that prison."

The princess informed
Her father the king, who
Promptly agreed to her proposal:
He then issued an edict
That allowed him to leave
And told the messenger
Not to dare tarry at all.
He was set free in a sec:
The rich man could go and leave!

        The rich man suffered quite an ordeal:
        Locked up in prison for eleven years!
        But once his son was a prince consort,
        He was saved and could leave his cell.

---

56. To be loyal means to be loyal to the ruling dynasty.

XXI. Little Huaxian Becomes Prince Consort and Saves His Father from Prison

[Pangzhuangtai]

A pain that was unbearable:
As the son longed for his mother, his tears coursed down.
"My mother suffers misery in the prison below the earth,
So her son can never be at ease, can never have any peace.
The family wealth of a million cannot be employed at all,
Who thought that father and son now could be reunited?
My heart filled with pain
I secretly thank Heaven:
Father and son have been able to be reunited on this day!"

[Plain prose] Tell that little Huaxian, having become a prince consort, saved his father from prison. After he had led him into the palace to express his thanks for this favor, Huaxian knelt down and said, "Your Majesty, please be informed that I have a stepmother, woman You, who with her hundredfold venomous mind bitterly tried to harm your subject." He told him the whole story from beginning to end. The court then proclaimed, "Prince consort, I give you three thousand troops to arrest those four enemies, that district magistrate, woman You, woman Kang, and the one who sold the poison." But no more about that.

Now tell that woman Yang in the underworld had finished embroidering the four red gauze precious curtains. The divinities were overjoyed and the Eldest Lad, the Second Lad, the Fourth Lad, and the Fifth Lad each added five more years to her life—originally she would have reached the age of seventy-two but now, with twenty years added, it would be ninety-two years. The Lads ordered their ghostly underlings to take woman Yang's true soul back so she could revive.

> Today woman Yang will come back to life
> To walk forward on the roads of this world.

Only when woman Yang
    Had passed Ghost Gate Pass[57]
        Did she see the sun in the sky:

---

57. Ghost Gate Pass is the entry to the underworld.

Dazzlingly clear,
   Brilliantly bright,
      This was a different cosmos!
Her dark spirit
   Followed the ghosts
      Who did not dare tarry at all,
And in a moment
   They had arrived
      In the village named Huaxian.
On entering the gate,
   They threw her soul
      Into the shell of the corpse,
When rich man Zhang,
   Leading his army,
      Also entered the house gate.
Leading three thousand
   Infantry and cavalry
      He encircled the dwelling
To arrest woman You,
   That no-good wife,
      And cut her to pieces and paste.
Tell that woman You,
   Flustered and flurried,
      Threw herself down on the ground
And called out, "My husband,
   And you, prince consort,
      Please be so kind as to spare my life,"
When they suddenly heard
   From inside the coffin
      Someone calling out loudly,
"Rich man Zhang,"
   Calling, "Prince Consort,"
      And all the others by name.
They all gathered
   Around the coffin,
      And heard it was no mistake:
They opened the coffin
   And helped woman Yang
      To step out of the coffin.

On seeing his mother
    That little Huaxian
        Clutched her in his arms,
And the rich man
    Could not stop himself
        From wailing most sadly.
After weeping a while
    Woman Yang said,
        "I have suffered greatly
And in the underworld
    For twelve long years
        I always longed for my boy."
The little Huaxian
    Knelt down in front
        Of his mother, and wept,
"Your son has suffered
    An all-encompassing punishment
        And barely survived with his life.
Your child was beaten
    By that stepmother
        In a hundred cruel ways:
Covered with thorns,
    Boiled in a wok:
        So did she try to do me in.
She had your son
    Eat some poison,
        So his whole body turned black,
But when the Third Lad
    Had saved my life,
        She conceived yet another plan:
She had made
    A sharp knife
        In order to kill your dear son,
But unexpectedly
    She killed by mistake
        The little boy that was her own.

She grabbed me tightly
And refuse to let me go:
She accused me of murder in court.

She paid a hundred taels:
When tortured, I confessed.
Condemned then to death
I was locked up in prison
But fortunately the Third Lad
Turned into a whirlwind
And lifted your son from the execution ground.

> My dear father broke the royal law,
> And condemned, was locked in jail.
> I, your child, had no other solution
> But to go begging for twelve years."

XXII. The Rich Man, His Wife, the Princess, and the Prince Consort Are Reunited

[Shanpoyang]
Of all people in the world
None suffered misfortune like our one family!
We all were, eyes wide-opened, dispersed and scattered.
Father and mother and child
Have almost been incapable of meeting each other again.
Escaping from death
We suffered innumerable tortures and punishments,
And who could have thought we today would be reunited?
Passing by the bunted loft the ball was thrown
And I was married to a princess.
Our bitter pain was inexpressible,
Our bitter pain was inexpressible,
So we prayed to Heaven;
Our bitter pain was inexpressible,
But now Heaven's retribution is clear to see!

[Plain prose] Tell that the whole family of the rich man, woman Yang, the prince consort, and the princess was gathered and reunited. After they had expressed their thanks to the gods, the prince consort told his mother the whole story, "The imperial court provided me with three thousand infantry and cavalry to arrest these four criminals and exact revenge. Woman You has already been arrested by me and is shackled in the front yard. Now we will also arrest woman Kang, the district magistrate, and the man who sold the poison. They will be taken to the Capital, but even if they are sliced to pieces by knives to repay them for that murder by poison, that would still not be enough to satisfy my desires." When woman Yang heard this she said, "Wonderful! But listen to your mother and set these four enemies free." The prince consort replied, "But my enmity with these four people is deeper than the sea. How can I forgive them?" Woman Yang replied, "If you do not listen to my advice, I will kill the two of you, so you never will be together." "Mother, don't act so rashly," the prince consort said, "I will pardon them all." Woman Yang kowtowed to express her thanks, and [the criminals] retreated shamefacedly.

> Her Ladyship woman Yang displayed great mercy,
> The prince consort and princess fully followed her.

That rich man Zhang
    Was one of heaven's
        Curtain-raising great generals,
And woman Yang
    Was a bodhisattva
        Who had been reborn as a human.
Little boy Huaxian
    Was a left golden boy
        Who was set to suffer misfortune;
The princess was
    A right jade maiden
        Who was born in the royal family.
That woman You was
    The Star of Destruction
        Who had descended to earth below;
The district magistrate
    Had broken the law
        Out of his lust for silver and cash.
Now the physician
    On seeing the silver
        Provided a package of poison,
And the whole world
    Called woman Kang
        A sweet-tongued glib talking hag.
If woman Yang urged
    To pardon the lives
        Of all these four criminal creatures

It was because eventually
  Heaven would destroy them:
    They'd never be reborn as humans!
This rich man Zhang
  Donated his wealth
    For repairing roads and building ways,
And swore an oath
  He would eat no meat,
    Recite Buddha's name, and read sutras.
Little Huaxian
  As a prince consort
    Was forbearing and observed purity;
The good princess
  Made many donations,
    Spreading her riches, feasting clerics.
These four bodhisattvas
  Turned the Dharma wheel,
    Unbeknownst to anyone here on earth,
And if I had not
  Pointed out the way,
    You would not have understood a bit.
Ask an enlightened teacher,
  Seek out friends in the Way,
    To know what are the Four Phenomena:[58]
All is vacuous emptiness;
  The Dharma World spreads throughout,
    Permeating the cosmos of Qian and Kun.[59]
The Mother carried you
  And she gave birth to you,
    All nine hundred and ninety thousand,
And after eighty kalpas
  We have arrived at the coming
    Congregation of the Dragon-Flower.
Arrived at this point
  You must let go
    And make yet another step forward:

---

58. The Four Phenomena refer to the four stages of all phenomena: birth, being, change (decay), and death.
59. Qian and Kun are the names of the first two hexagrams of the *Book of Changes* and stand here for Yin and Yang.

Cross the Dark Gate,
    Surpass the three realms,[60]
        And return to your fate and your roots.
I urge this assembly
    Not to miss the opportunity
        Of the great meaning from the West:
At Maitreya's
    Dragon-Flower Assembly
        You'll achieve a second body of gold.

When the ceremony was completed
The four deities returned to heaven:
Their true natures went to the Spirit Peak.[61]
The precious scroll has been chanted,
Find peace in the Buddhist sutras.
We wish our Imperial King a sage life of millions,
A sage life of millions of years.
The Dharma World is responsive.
So may we all ascend to the Heaven of Ultimate Bliss.[62]

Hail to the *Single Vehicle School, Limitless Meaning, True Vacuity Miraculous Sutra on Deliverance from Suffering by the Tathāgata*

Transfer [the merit of this ceremony] to the unsurpassable bodhi[63] of the Buddha

Prostrate I wish that the sound of the sutra may have loudly and clearly penetrated to the heavenly halls up above, and pierced the dark and dank offices in the earth down below. May those who recite the name of the Buddha depart from the Three Paths[64] and the Prisons below the Earth; may those who commit evil for kalpas on end fall away from the spiritual light, and may those who have obtained enlightenment be led on their way by the Buddhas, emitting a clear light that shines on all ten directions. May in east and west the returning light shine backwards, and in south and north each personally arrive at his

---

60. The three realms are the realm of sensuous desire, the realm of pure form, and the realm of pure spirit.
61. The Spirit Peak is the place where the Buddha preached many of his most important sutras.
62. The Heaven of Ultimate Bliss refers to the Western Paradise of the Buddha Amitābha.
63. Bodhi is the wisdom that leads to enlightenment.
64. The Three Paths refer to the path of misery, the path of action producing karma, and the resulting path of suffering.

home. Board the floating boat of the Unborn to reach the shore, and the little infants will be reunited with their own mother. Once inside the mother's womb you don't have to fear the three disasters, you will join the Dragon-Flower for the eighty-first kalpa, and for all eternity enjoy peace and prosperity.

At that moment the four gods, rich man Zhang and his wife woman Yang, together with Little Huaxian and the Cuihua[65] princess, returned to heaven.

> If sins emerge from the heart, repent in your heart;
> If the heart is annihilated, the sin is also forgotten.
> Sin forgotten, heart annihilated—both are empty:
> This makes clear that the repentance was sincere.
>
> All multiple evil karma of the sins we committed
> Lasts from the Unbeginning down to the present.
> Banished from Spirit Peak, your true nature is lost
> But one spark of spiritual light links all beings.[66]
>
> May you now like this all convert [to the truth],
> Return to your original root and experience bodhi.
> Grasp the great Way, and once truly enlightened,
> You'll joyfully join the Dragon-Flower Assembly.

> First of all, let us repay Heaven and Earth's favor of covering and carrying;
> Secondly let us repay the sun and moon's favor of shining their light on us;
> Thirdly let us repay the Imperial King's favor of giving us water and earth;
> Fourthly let us repay our father and mother's favor of feeding and raising us.

> Each and every Buddha of the ten directions and the three worlds;
> The bodhisattvas Mañjuśrī and Guanyin,
> All bodhisattvas and mahāsattvas,
> And the Mahā-prajñāpāramitā.

The end of the Precious Scroll of the Red Gauze as Preached by the Buddha

Printed and published by the bookseller Wu Yangquan

---

65. The name of the princess was earlier given as Cuiwei.
66. The "one spark of spiritual being" refers to the Buddha nature that is present in all beings. The term here translated as "all beings" refers to the four classes of beings as differentiated by their manner of birth.

The *Precious Scroll, as Preached by the Buddha, of the Handkerchief: How Wang Zhongqing Lost Everything*

The Hymn for Raising the Incense

>The precious scroll, wrapped in a kerchief,
>Descends to the dharma world here below.
>The bodhisattva ferries across all living beings
>And awakens the people of this secular realm.
>Throughout the past and the present
>The words of the sutras are perfectly the same.

Hail to the Bodhisattva Mahāsattva who saves from sufferings and disasters! *(The community repeats this three times.)*

The Gatha for Opening the Scroll

>The unsurpassable and unfathomable subtle and wonderful Dharma
>Is rarely encountered in a hundred thousands of millions of kalpas.
>Now I today have seen it and heard it and can receive and uphold it,
>I desire to understand the Tathāgata's true and substantial meaning.

Hail to the Three Treasures of Buddha, Dharma and Sangha of the Past, the Present, and the Future that, Utterly Void, Pervade the dharma world!

I have heard about a case of cause and fruit that occurred during the present dynasty[1] in our country. It concerns bodhisattvas and arhats who descended to the mortal world.

In the old days there was a village called Sanxian, also known as Bali Hamlet, outside the Eastern Capital, the city of Bian of the state of Liang.[2] There lived a rich man, a local notable, who was called Wang Zhongqing. His wife Zhang Suzhen from birth loved good deeds, and from her earliest years maintained the fast; she read the sutras and recited the name of the Buddha, feasted monks, and distributed donations, widely forming good karma. Now Wang Zhongqing's heart was not pious, so he said to his wife, "The ancients put it very well: A family may have a thousand strings of cash, but if there is no daily income [it will not suffice]. When you feast those monks and hand out donations, we have only expenses and no returns. Drink some more good wine and eat some more good meat, to satiate and feed the four elements,[3] and to enrich and strengthen the body; dress yourself in satin and silk to enhance the impression you make. To keep the fast and follow a vegetarian diet will only uselessly harm your five organs and their six gods."[4]

    When Suzhen had heard this, she secretly heaved a sigh:
    The struggle for fame and pursuit of profit is all in vain!

"My dear husband,
    Please listen to me
        And let me explain it in full:
These four elements
    Will decompose
        Into a hole of shit and piss.
[The human body]
    Will not last long,
        [Death may arrive any day,]
[So I pray] you
    To quickly convert
        And use the fake to seek truth.[5]

---

1. Che Xilun suggests the reading 金 for 今, which would turn "the present dynasty" into "the Jin dynasty." It is more likely that the story is set in the Northern Song dynasty.
2. The text actually says "the city of Liang of the state of Bian." This refers to Kaifeng, the capital of the Northern Song dynasty.
3. The four elements that make up the body (earth, water, fire, and wind).
4. The five organs refer to liver, heart, spleen, lungs, and kidneys; the six gods refer to the divinities of these five organs and the gall bladder.
5. The phrases in brackets in these two lines are illegible in the Ming manuscript and have been inserted based on the context. "The fake" here refers to one's ephemeral existence as a human being.

During their lifetime
   People scheme in vain
      To amass gold and collect jade,
But truly alas,
   The unfeeling
      Sun and moon urge you on.
In vain you collect
   Millions of taels,[6]
      But silver and gold have no use:
When Death arrives
   You will find out
      That all your labor was useless."
When rich man Wang
   Had heard these words,
      He replied in the following way,
"By keeping the fast
   You wrongly harm
      The five organs, their six gods.
All day long
   You keep the fast
      But feast and fatten the monks,
Yet when Death arrives,
   You too can't escape
      Going down to the underworld."

Woman Zhang pleaded and urged
Her husband to quickly turn around,
But the rich man grew only more furious,
"When one dies, there is no return,
What is this nonsense about rebirth?
As long as we're wealthy and noble,
We should truly enjoy ourselves!
Once Death comes and fetches us,
Everything will be over and done."

      When Suzhen heard him say these words
      She bowed her head, thinking to herself,
      "The Buddha's Dharma may be wonderful,
      But it is hard to persuade a single person."

---

6. A tael is one ounce of silver.

I. Zhang Suzhen Urges Her Husband to Convert and Devote Himself to the Way, but He Refuses to Do So

[Huameixu]

In this world of red dust
We hurry and run in vain:
You vaunt your strength in the struggle for fame and pursuit of profit
And don't fear at all that King Yama will have you arrested and taken—
A single dream of yellow millet![7]
Gone to the underworld
You will never come back home:
In vain you remember the features of your sons and daughters—
How sad!
Against the sufferings of hell there exists no barrier or defense:
The prison of iron beds even surpasses vats of seething water,
Surpasses vats of seething water!

Tell that Zhang Suzhen heaved a heavy sigh. She waited till the next morning to tell her husband, "I have something I want to discuss with you." Her husband replied, "Feel free to say whatever you want." Suzhen then said, "I am presently very much concerned about life and death. If I mistakenly pass by the Message Arrived from the West,[8] in which kalpa and in which year will I appear again? When I urge you to abstain from alcohol and meat, you absolutely refuse to do so, and from morning till late you vent your spleen on me, so my own body does not remain clear and pure and the sutras and images are befouled. This is really too bad. You should marry another woman and bring her home as your wife. First of all, she can serve you; secondly, she can take care of the servants and the guests; and thirdly, she can manage the household affairs for me, so I can devote myself to my piety without distraction."

>When her husband heard her say this, he secretly thought,
>"I say goodbye to this sutra-reading, Buddha-reciting wife!"

---

7. A "yellow millet dream" is a dream that awakens one to the illusionary nature of all earthly riches and glory. The allusion is based on a well-known tale from the Tang dynasty: When passing through the city of Handan a young man on his way to the capital to take the exams stops at an inn and falls asleep, waiting for his meal of yellow millet porridge to be cooked. In a dream he experiences a long and successful official career with all its ups and downs, but when he wakes up, it turns out that the yellow millet still has not been cooked. Awakened to the illusionary nature of existence, the young man abandons his ambition.

8. The "Message Arrived from the West" is Buddhism. Buddhism entered China by way of Central Asia, so from the west.

Tell that the rich man
   Went out of his house,
      Filled with despondent feelings;
Walking the flower streets
   As well as the willow lanes[9]
      He tried to find some distraction.
Together with
   A rich man Zhang
      He entered into one of the houses
Where they found
   Third Sister Li
      Who was living there all by herself.
Rich man Wang
   Often came
      To her place to have a drink with her,
"At home my wife,
   That Zhang Suzhen,
      Keeps to the fast, devoted to piety.
She doesn't administer
   The household affairs
      As she is set on self-cultivation,
So she ordered me
   To marry another wife
      To take care of the household."
When Third Sister Li
   Heard him say this,
      She smiled to him with a sneer,
But rich man Wang
   Was fully determined
      To marry as wife this woman Li.
Now this woman Li
   Also wanted to wed
      A man who was very wealthy,
So rich man Zhang
   Acted as go-between;
      This day was extremely lucky!
That very moment
   He brought woman Li
      Into his house as his new wife,

---

9. "Flower streets" and "willow lanes" are both euphemisms for brothel districts.

And when he came home
   The whole household
      Was happily smiling for joy.

Entering the gate, she made a bow
Before Zhang Suzhen, who thought
"This fake manner, this fake person,
This demon spirit, this demon fiend
Really scares one out of one's mind!"
In her heart she secretly pondered,
"If I would have to evaluate them,
My husband is way too old
For this girl, who is still quite young!"

      Zhang Suzhen told her husband,
       "You truly have no shame at all!
       At your age marrying this girl—
       People will all call you a fool."

II. When Woman Zhang Said This, Woman Li Conceived Evil Thoughts on Hearing It

[Zhufeiyun]
Secretly she gnashed her teeth,
"You may read sutras, but your mind is amiss.
The two families were in agreement,
You repeatedly came to speak to me.
Damned woman, how stupid you are,
What a nuisance!
You and I have become enemies from now on,
And I will slowly find a way to have revenge,
To have revenge!"

Tell that woman Li became the sworn enemy of Suzhen from the moment she entered the house. She had stayed there for some days—but no more about that.

Now tell that Suzhen might be intelligent, but she had no clue of what was going on, so she told woman Li, "I am someone who keeps to the fast and have no mind to take care of the household affairs. Now you have come to our family, I will hand the keys of all chambers over to you, but there are two things you have to do for me." Woman Li replied, "Just tell me which two things. I am listening."

    Suzhen stepped forward and addressed her as follows,
   "Dear sister, please listen and I will explain this clearly."

"The first thing is
  That when monks and clerics
    Come to ask for a donation from me,
Then get out as much
  As I told you to do—
    In this you definitely have to obey me.
The second thing is
  That in preparing vegetarian food,
    You must be sincere, clear, and pure.
If the two of us
  Both joyfully make the donation,
    Of course we are bound to succeed."
This woman Li
  Said, "Dear sister,
    I have heard what you told me.
Each and every sentence
  Of what you just said
    I have memorized in my heart.
I'll manage the house,
  I will cook the food,
    Welcome the guests and servants,
While you, undistracted,
  Recite the true sutras,
    Make donations, and feast monks."
Having said this,
  This woman Li
    Strode out of the room and left,
While Zhang Suzhen
  In her Buddha chapel
    Recited the text of the sutras.
She really was hoping,
  Escaping once and for all,
    To transcend the three realms

And had no clue
>She had invited misfortune
>>By inciting the Star of Disaster!

In her sutra chapel our Suzhen,
Loudly reciting the true sutras,
Handed out donations and feasted monks.
The gate of goodness is easily opened,
The gate of goodness is hard to close.
But woman Li thought to herself,
"That woman Zhang, that Suzhen,
Feasts monks and makes donations,
Bossing me around without a moment of rest!"

>Woman Li darkly thought to herself,
>"Good people are too easily abused.
>If I do not put in an effort right now,
>I will end up being bossed around."

III. When Preparing Food for Monks, Woman Li Feels Aggravated beyond Endurance

[Zhuyunfei]

Her heart was filled with vexation,
"All day long she lets me have no moment of rest:
I prepare the tea and also cook the rice,
She bosses me around so I cannot stop and pause.
But if there is something unsupportable,
How can I open my mouth?
If our husband hears her talk
And I don't chime in,
I have to do as she says,
Or he'll make a mess of the house,
Or he'll make a mess of the house!"

Tell that woman Li was pondering the situation in her heart—but no more of it.

Now tell that Zhang Suzhen called her son Wang Tianlu over to her, and said, "Bring your father with you to the sutra chapel." Suzhen then told her husband, "I've learned that you and woman Li are staying in the eastern house, so I will take Wang Tianlu and my daughter Huixiang with me and live in the western house. I will there read the sutras and recite the name of the Buddha, so I can be at ease, not disturbed by anyone." When her husband heard this, he replied to her, "Do as you want, you are free to do so." As soon as he had said so, he took a servant along and left to collect accounts, but no more about that.

Now tell that after a while a group of monks arrived, begging for food. They recited their sutras in front of the gate from break of dawn, but even by noon they still had received no rice. On top of that woman Li came outside and told them, "My husband is right now quite strict. He was afraid that his wealth was squandered and married me to manage his household affairs. We don't feast monks anymore, and the gate for the wise has been closed. He has packed off the main wife Suzhen to the western house to live there by herself."

When the monks heard this, they heaved a sigh:
The gate had been truly closed once and for all.

These many monks
 Next all arrived
  In front of the western house;
Raising and beating
 Their wooden fishes,[10]
  They recited the Diamond Sutra.
Now Zhang Suzhen
 Was seated upright
  In meditation in her sutra chapel,
When she suddenly heard
 The wooden fish sound,
  So she went over to have a look.
When she saw the monks,
 She was filled with joy,
  Inclining her body to make a bow,
And she stepped forward
 To ask these monks
  For what purpose they had come.
"You must have come
 To beg for a vegetarian meal
  Or perhaps for some donation,

---

10. A wooden fish is a fish-shaped hollowed-out piece of wood used as a percussion instrument in Buddhist rituals.

So I ask you, masters,
   To follow me inside,
      Have a seat in the sutra chapel."
These dhyana monks
   Followed Suzhen
      And sat down in the sutra chapel,
And with one voice
   Started to recite
      All chapters of the holy sutras.
When Suzhen
   Heard their voices,
      Her heart was filled with joy.
"I now will go
   To the eastern house
      To order some food for you all."
When Zhang Suzhen
   Came to the eastern house
      She loudly called for woman Li,
"Please hurry up
   And prepare some food
      So I can feed all those monks!"

When woman Li heard this,
She was overcome by rage,
And she deeply pondered this in her heart.
Then she said, "Dear sister,
Now listen to what I'll say.
Our husband has yesterday
Told me in very clear words:
Closed is the gate for the wise.
He doesn't want you to feed those monks!

      Our husband has made up his mind:
      You don't need to feed those monks!
      But out of the blue you blame me—
         I cannot prepare vegetarian food!"

IV. When Zhang Suzhen Hears This, Tears Course Down from Her Eyes as She Returns to the Western House

[Jinzijing]
Suzhen's tears coursed down in streams,
"Offering a vegetarian meal
From now on depends on that evil person.
Her hindrance closes the gate for the wise—
How insupportable!
How insupportable!
The handles of power are not in my hands!"

Tell that Zhang Suzhen ordered woman Li to prepare a vegetarian meal and that she refused to do so. When she asked for rice to give the monks a vegetarian meal, she simply didn't give it. So Suzhen had no other option but to borrow some cups of rice from others. After she had cooked some rice, she distributed it among the monks, who left after eating it—but no more about that.

Now tell that Suzhen was awash in tears, worried and depressed. When not much later Wang Tianlu came home from school and saw that his mother looked anxious, he stepped forward and asked her, "Mother, what are you so anxious about?" Suzhen then told her son, "Initially, I know, I myself proposed that he should marry her so she could in my place look after household affairs and serve your father, and I could with a settled mind devote myself to piety and prepare for my future. But who could have thought that that woman Li would now refuse to obey me? When yesterday some monks arrived begging for a vegetarian meal, she didn't obey me. When I told her to cook some rice, she said that I was impossible, and when I asked her for some cups of rice, she refused to give it to me. All these monks had heard our name, and had been informed that our family practices good deeds, so they came from afar to appeal to us. But they didn't even get one full meal of rice, so they left filled with anger. So what is now the benefit of all my keeping to the fast and reciting the name of the Buddha? That's why I am so anxious." When Wang Tianlu had heard this, he cried out, "Mother, that woman Li is nothing more than a slave under your command. If she offends you like this, can't you give her a beating? My sister and I will go over there and haul her here, and then you administer a beating with a big club!" On hearing this, Suzhen said, "That would release my rage!"

> If I now show some mercy and kindness and don't take a stand,
> I'll only stiffen that no-good house-wrecking slut in her attitude.

THE *PRECIOUS SCROLL OF THE HANDKERCHIEF* 111

Mother and children,
    Their heart filled with rage,
        Arrived at the eastern mansion,
And loudly shouted,
    "Where are you,
        That no-good spouse woman Li?
Because our family
    Was short of servants,
        We brought you here as a bride,
But you this
    Lowly slave
        Are too brazen and treacherous.
When I feed monks
    Or hand out donations,
        My actions conform to the rules,
But when I give an order
    And you don't obey me,
        You close my gate for the wise."
Now this woman Li
    Relied on her husband,
        And brazenly acted most daring
By vilifying
    Zhang Suzhen
        Who recited the name of the Buddha.
Wang Tianlu
    And his sister Huixiang
        Tightly got hold of woman Li
Who had enraged
    Her sutra-reading
        Goodness-loving mistress
Who took to hand
    A thick cudgel
        And raised it high in the air,
Then brought it down
    On this no-good slut,
        Cruelly, without any mercy!
One after another
    She gave tens of strokes
        To a painfully suffering woman Li,

Who butted with her head into,
    And with her hands held onto
        That woman Zhang, that Suzhen.
"I will today
    Lose my life
        At the hands of mother and children!"
With hair unbound
    And scratched cheeks
        She cried out her pain without end.

Suzhen cursed her out
For a no-good woman,
"You refuse to obey the orders I give!
Make a scene, rotten carrion!
Too brazen! Too treacherous!
When counting out all things,
I take you for a resting cloud![11]
Because you a moment ago
Treated me like I am a stranger to you!"

        Taking along her son and her daughter
        She returned to her sutra-reading chapel.
        Woman Li wept, howling and hollering,
        Lying on the ground in the courtyard.

V. When Woman Li Saw That Suzhen Had Left, She Undid Her Hair and Rolled About

[Zhumating]

Filled with a furious rage
She vilified that sutra-reading Suzhen,
"You mother and children,
Were too mean and tricky
To give me such a beating!
How can I now ever let go of this hatred?
This cruel beating was truly unbearable!
How much time did it take?

---

11. An ephemeral object of no value.

Disconsolate and anxious
I can only give up my life!"

Tell that woman Li, this ladyship, was rolling about on the ground with her hair unbound and all in a mess, occupied by her vexations.

Now tell that the rich man came home from collecting accounts and saw woman Li rolling about on the ground, weeping and howling. As soon as the rich man saw this, he asked, "Woman Li, how did you get in this state?" Woman Li replied, "My husband, you have to know that as soon as you had left to collect accounts, monks and clerics kept on clamoring at the gate, and when they had received a vegetarian meal, they demanded donations. She also kept them at her western mansion, where they stayed for three or four days. They were talking, they were laughing, so I could not but notice them. When I spoke to her about it, it was with the best of intentions. If you want to feast monks and make donations like this, you would waste your fortune even if you had tens of thousands of ounces of yellow gold! But she said, 'This is none of your business. This is all capital that I brought into the wedding.' So that's fine with me. But, husband, your name is known throughout the world and pervades all regions. If you enjoy such fame, but monks and clerics stay with your wife in a manner that people cannot but notice, then you become a laughingstock to your neighbors, won't you? So I pointed out some of her faults, but she said that I gave myself airs, and then her two children held me down and she got a cudgel and administered me a beating, almost beating me to death. She has been your wife since your youth and I am a woman without champion, so I wanted to wait until you had arrived so I could explain this to you, and then commit suicide."

> On hearing this, the rich man's heart was filled with a furious rage
> And he loudly shouted, "My wife, you acted without any feeling!"

Tell that the rich man
   Got out a cudgel
      And went out through the gate.
Within a short while
   He had arrived
      Inside the other, western house.
He did not talk
   About any small things
      But grabbed his wife tightly;
Raising his club
   He wildly beat
      That woman Zhang, Suzhen.

The two children
   Held on to their father,
      Howling and hollering, weeping,
And called to their father,
   "Please don't beat
      The mother that bore both of us!"
But the old rich man
   Didn't listen at all
      To the prayers of his children
And for better or worse
   Kept on beating and whipping
      That woman who recited sutras.
He gave Zhang Suzhen
   Such a terrible beating
      Her head was covered in blood,
As he loudly shouted,
   "What kind of fast?
      What kind of sutra-recitation?
All day long
   You give our money
      As donations to begging monks.
If we all act like you
   How would we eventually
      Still be able to feed ourselves?
Now if I see you
   One more time
      Feed monks and make donations,
I swear you will
   Lose your life
      At my hands!"

In her anxiety Suzhen
Addressed the deities,
"Mishap and misfortune all in this existence!
Now I'm filled with regret,
But who could have known?
It was I who proposed she
Could deal with the guests,
And I never thought that I
Would stir up the fire that burns my body!"

Suzhen grew even more anxious,
"I made the wrong decision back then."
Mother and children could only sigh:
The rich man had sided with *her*.

VI. After the Rich Man Has Given Suzhen a Beating, He Returns to the Eastern House

[Zaoluopao]

Inside the Buddha chapel
I want to recite my sutras,
But involuntarily tears course down like a spring:
My present sufferings are due to my former lives.
Dragons and devas up in the sky,
You are my witnesses
That my whole body is hurting,
That all of my body is bruised.
Life and death is a major issue,
Mishap and misfortune a minor—
Suddenly I hear outside the sound of sutra-recitation.

Tell that while Zhang Suzhen was caught up in her anxieties, again some monks had arrived, begging for food. When Suzhen heard the sound of the wooden fishes, she went out of the gate and saw there two poor monks: they were clad in tatters, and their haggard faces were sallow from hunger. When Suzhen saw them, she was deeply moved, and her tears resembled a gushing spring. "These two masters definitely must have come from afar. Now they appeal to me today, I don't know whether they are begging for food of for clothes to cover their bodies. But the handles of power are not in my hands right now." But as she found it impossible to suppress her heart, she walked forward and asked them, "Masters, what are you begging for?" The poor monks replied, "Some hundreds of miles away we learned of your good heart and lofty fame. Today we appeal to you and beg you for clothes to cover our bodies so we may bow before the Buddha on your behalf." Suzhen then answered, "Dear masters, I am not a stingy person. But my husband is very strict and not altruistic, and recently he has married a concubine woman Li, who is extremely evil. When yesterday some monks had arrived, I told her to cook some rice, but she altogether refused to do so, and when I asked her for some cups of rice, she also refused to give any to me. When I got angry and hit her a few times, she ran off to my husband and greatly embellished her story, so my husband administered me a beating, almost beating me to death!"

   When Suzhen had said this, she felt even more troubled,
   Because that rotten slut had closed the gate for the wise.

Zhang Suzhen
 Pulled out a golden hairpin
  And addressed them as follows,
"You[12] hand this over
 To those two masters—
  The gate for the wise has been closed.
Buy some clothes
 With this hairpin,
  Dear masters, to cover your bodies.
From my earliest youth
 I have kept to the fast,
  But all that effort is without result."
Once she had said so,
 Those two monks
  Departed on their long wanderings,
And Zhang Suzhen
 Returned to the sutra chapel,
  Her eyes all awash in tears.
Filled with anxiety
 She once again
  Loudly recited the sutras,
Her only intention
 Being that she wanted
  To escape from the world of red dust.
Mother and children
 Could do nothing
  But pray to Heaven and Earth
That all evil people
 Might be far removed
  And they might meet pious people.

Mother and children in the sutra chapel
Were all awash in tears as they thought,

---

12. Suzhen is here speaking to a servant girl or her daughter.

"We lack good karma from former existences,
So in this life our lord and master
Is completely without any virtue:
He believes in all her machinations,
And doesn't create any good karma.
Despite a capital of many millions
He still may end up completely empty-handed."

When Suzhen abandoned her anxious thoughts,
She recited the sutras of the Great Vehicle.
Repenting for the sins of interminable kalpas,
She burst from the immersion in suffering.

VII. While Zhang Suzhen and Her Children Are Caught Up by Anxious Thoughts, the Rich Man Comes Home as Drunk as Can Be

[Zhuyunfei]

Wealthy in cash and in grain,
I wake up in meat and doze off in wine:
Who is as carefree as me?
My life is far better than that of those bureaucrats,
My Heaven,
It surpasses that of the immortals,
So untrammeled it is!
Dressed in brocade and silk
I cruise the willow lanes and flower streets.
Once gone, one's lusty spring will not return,
Will not return!

Tell that Wang Zhongqing one day had had so much wine that he was as drunk as a skunk. When he came home, he was welcomed by woman Li, and the rich man asked her, "Have there been any monks or clerics coming to the house?" Woman Li replied, "My husband, things are not good." When the rich man asked, "How come not good?" woman Li said, "Early in the morning today there arrived two monks and in front of the gate they begged for donations. That Zhang Suzhen did not let me hear anything about it, she says that I have closed her gate for the wise. She also had quite a lot to say about you, and as she was talking she gnashed her teeth and pulled a couple of hairpins from her hairdo, which she gave to these two monks to come back with some more people. In one way or another, she wants to do the two of us in. I said to myself that if she truly was someone who tried to be a good person, what kind of deep enmity could she harbor even if you administered her a beating? What should we do now [if] all of a sudden she wants to team up with some bandits to do us in?"

> When the rich man heard this story he was quite furious
> And he repeatedly cursed his wife out as a damned slut.

When rich man Wang
   Had heard this story,
      He was filled with a furious rage
And cried, "Dear wife,
   Don't be concerned,
      Please set all your worries aside!"
While still in the thrall
   Of that furious rage,
      Not thinking about right or wrong,
He came, heavily panting,
   To the western mansion,
      Vilifying his "hairpins and skirt."
When he also saw
   That Zhang Suzhen
      Was missing that pair of hairpins,
He ran forward
   And tightly grasped
      The woman who recited the name of the Buddha.
Wang Tianlu
   And his sister Huixiang
      Loudly wept at the top of their voices
And held on to
   Their old father,
      Their eyes all awash in hot tears.
Because the rich man
   Was held back by
      His son and also his daughter,
He could not beat her,
   And grew even more furious,
      Became even more filled with rage.

Now Zhang Suzhen
   Had no defense
      Against her husband's second beating;
She only lowered her head,
   Gave free rein to her tears,
      And sadly wept at the top of her voice.
Overcome by rage
   The rich man once again
      Tightly grabbed his wife Zhang Suzhen,
Stretched a hand
   And ripped out
      One of her eyes.
Spattered with blood,
   Holding it in his hands,
      He returned to the eastern mansion
And left Suzhen
   Overcome by pain,
      Repeatedly calling out her suffering.
The whole socket
   Was filled with blood
      As she raised her voice and wept,
While the two children
   Supported their mother—
      Bereft of courage, fear-stricken.
"Of course I wanted
   To keep to the fast,
      Find an escape by self-cultivation,
But who could have known
   That now at present
      All my efforts would have no result."

Suzhen tightly held on to
Her son and her daughter,
And thought with a sigh, "How miserable!
I didn't understand at all
I lit the fire that burns me.
I thought I could at ease
Work on my future birth.
But since that slut came,
The gate for the wise is closed."

> The two of them, her son and daughter,
> Closely guarded their beloved mother.
> The piercing pain was truly unbearable
> And this alerted the King of Medicine.[13]

VIII. The King of Medicine Bodhisattva Healed Zhang Suzhen's Eye in a Dream

[Huameixu]
The whole socket was filled with blood:
This alerted the gods passing through the empty air.
"I will now collect the clouds and push away mists
And save and deliver all living beings."
While Zhang Suzhen would appear to be in a haze,
The old bodhisattva addressed her,
"I have researched your misery,
And your evil karma from prior kalpas is heavy,
But with this magic medicine you'll be fine everywhere!"

Tell that when Suzhen had wept until the third watch and finally had closed her eyes, she dreamed that a bodhisattva came and healed her eye. But when she woke up, it was only a Southern Bough dream.[14] But there came no blood out of her eye socket anymore and she also felt no pain. She saw that her two children were snoring away, as loud as the thunder! "Even though they are asleep, they are still holding on to my clothes." As she silently thought this, tears gushed from her eyes. "I am bound to die at the hands of that woman Li, so I will seek a way out first thing in the morning." In his dream Wang Tianlu called out to his mother, "Don't leave me and my sister behind! It is no big deal that you want to leave, but our father believes the words of woman Li, and who will be our champion when he beats us to death?" While talking the two children continued to sleep.

> When Suzhen heard her child speak in his dream,
> A knife pierced her breast—she was filled by pain.

---

13. The King of Medicine is the King of Medicine Bodhisattva (Bhaisajvaraja).
14. A Southern Bough dream is an illusionary dream. In a well-known tale from the Tang dynasty, a drunken man falls asleep and experiences a splendid career as the prefect of Southern Bough. When he wakes up, he learns that the setting of his dream had been the ant hill below the southern branch of the huge acacia tree in his courtyard.

When she saw her children
>   As they slept on the bed,
>   >   Her heart seemed as smothered by knives,
"Who understands
>   What kind of karma
>   >   Is enwrapping my whole body right now?
If I do not find
>   At break of dawn
>   >   A way to get out of this household,
I will be bound
>   To lose my life
>   >   At the evil hands of that woman Li."
Shedding hot tears
>   She went to the sutra chapel
>   >   To bow and say goodbye to the Buddha,
"Now when I today
>   Will have left this house,
>   >   Who will visit here and burn incense?"
Having made her bows,
>   She also went into
>   >   The room where she had been sleeping,
And as she observed
>   Her son and daughter,
>   >   A myriad of arrows pierced her heart.
She called, "My son,
>   Your mother today
>   >   Has no way out but to abandon you.
When you wake up
>   And look for me,
>   >   All you'll be able to grasp is thin air.
Of course I find it
>   Hard to do without
>   >   Orchid rooms and painted pavilions.
I suffer for my son
>   And I suffer for my daughter—
>   >   These sighs are killing my heart.
I carry a grudge
>   Against my mean husband
>   >   Who believes all woman Li says

And has forgotten
    That earlier, youthful
        Affection of husband and wife."
Weeping she went
    And weeping she returned,
        Once again watching her kids,
"The two of them
    Are fast asleep,
        Filling my heart with a fright.
But if I right now
    Out of love for my children
        Fail to cut off that affection,
Then it may well be
    That I in the morning
        Will be unable to save my life."
She wept for a while
    And then steeled her heart
        To cut off all love and affection,
And as painful tears
    Coursed down from her eyes,
        She went to the garden behind.

Piteously she prayed to the sky,
The coming and going deities,
"Take pity on this Buddha-reciting person!
Please guide me on a clear way
To a good place to live in peace."
Again pained by her children
She found it so hard to depart,
And climbing across the wall,
Overcome by emotions she loudly wept.

> The heart of Suzhen now had been awakened:
> She jumped out of the hole of good and bad.
> Understanding the sufferings of the red dust,
> She, for better or worse, proved the Unborn.[15]

---

15. She freed herself from all attachments to devote herself to the eternal truth of Buddhism.

IX. Zhang Suzhen Escaped from the Flower Garden behind the House, and Where She Traveled Fleeing for Her Life

[Lanhua Ganzhou]

Suzhen in her anxiety prayed to dragons and devas,
"When will I come back now I leave home today?"
Planets move and stars turn as a cold wind blows,
I'm so cold that I'm shaking like winnowing chaff.
As I think of my dear son, tears gush from my eyes.
When I turn back to look
He is really quite pitiable.
In what region will I be able to settle down in peace?
I slowly move on,
Each step is harder.
Both the fast and Buddha-recitation were all in vain,
Were all in vain!

Tell that Zhang Suzhen had left home and was on the road, overcome by vexation—but no more about that.

Now tell that when Wang Tianlu suddenly woke up, he did not see his mother, which gave him quite a scare. He hurried to the sutra chapel and repeatedly called out her name, but no one answered. Weeping at the top of his voice he returned to the bedroom, where he woke up his sister Huixiang, "Don't pretend you're asleep and dreaming. Our mother has run off to god knows where. I went to the sutra chapel to look, but there was no trace." When his sister Huixiang so suddenly was awakened and heard her brother's voice, she was quite startled and called to her brother, "I'm only afraid that our father came again to administer a beating to our mother."

> The couple of brother and sister were flustered and flurried,
> Overcome by vexations because she had left without a trace.

"This must mean
   That our mother
      Has abandoned us here.
If that is the case
   On whom should we
      For better or worse rely?"

They sought quite long,
>   But found no trace
>   >   And wept at the top of their voices;
The elder brother
>   Tightly held his sister,
>   >   Bereft of courage, fear-stricken!
They also searched
>   The back flower garden,
>   >   But even there found no trace,
So they loudly cried,
>   "You cruel mother
>   >   Have abandoned your children.
The mother who bore us
>   Suffered such misery,
>   >   But who is there to understand?
We can only resent
>   Our own father
>   >   For cutting off all his affection."

They wept in the back rooms,
They wailed in the front hall,
With each voice calling out, "Dear mother,
You abandoned your children,
How are we going to survive?
That cruel-hearted father, he
Is really bereft of all feeling:
He only believes woman Li,
Who is a house-wrecking no-good slut!"

>   >   The children howled and hollered and wept:
>   >   At that time it was during the third watch.
>   >   They sought their mother but found no trace
>   >   And wept till the morning brightly broke.

X. Wang Tianlu and His Sister Huixiang Fail to Find Any Trace of Their Mother

[Yue'ergao]

When they came to the sutra chapel,
They quickly lighted one of the lamps.

The sutra-table was there as before
But they saw no trace of their mother.
Their hearts were cut by knives,
Their hearts were cut by knives,
As tears gushed down.
Now their mother was far away,
Who on earth was going to be their parent?
On whom to rely now their mother had left them?
Stamping their feet and beating their breasts
They anxiously wept at the top of their voices,
They anxiously wept at the top of their voices.

Now tell that Wang Tianlu and his sister Huixiang were in shock at a loss for what to do and could only give in to their anxiety—but no more about that.

Now tell that the rich man only awoke from his stupor after he had slept till the fourth watch. Suddenly he heard the two children piteously weeping in their anxiety without ever dropping their voices, so he was quite alarmed in his heart and asked woman Li, "How come that at this hour we still don't hear Zhang Suzhen reciting her sutras, and that I only hear those children weeping and wailing?" Woman Li replied, "Husband, have you forgotten everything? Last night you were drunk, and I don't know what Zhang Suzhen did to you when you went to the western house, but you wanted to give her a beating, and when the children held on to you and you could not beat her, you ripped out one of her eyes." When the rich man heard this, he was greatly alarmed, and shouted to woman Li, "Don't fool me!" But she said, "If you don't believe me, that eye is still here on this tray. I didn't throw it away."

When the rich man heard this story, all color drained from his face;
Stamping his feet and beating his breast he emitted sad lamentations.

He cried out, "My son,
  Where may your mother
    Now have gone to hide herself?"
Wang Tianlu
  And his sister Huixiang
    Held on to their father's body.
When he in all hurry
  Had arrived at the western house
    Inside the sutra-reading chapel,

He there saw
>   His two children
>   >   Piteously weeping, overcome by grief.

They called out,
>   "You cruel father
>   >   Believed the words of woman Li!

To which place
>   Have you packed away
>   >   Our mother to spend her days?

How could you
>   Rip out the left
>   >   Eye of our dear darling mother?

Your heart
>   Was utterly cruel
>   >   Not to think of your former love!

When earlier
>   She likewise
>   >   Fed the monks and gave donations,

Mules and horses were many,
>   Money and goods were plenty,
>   >   And all people were living at peace.

She and you
>   Together had us
>   >   As your children, a boy and a girl.

But you don't care
>   About our dear mother
>   >   And treat us without any feeling."

The two children
>   Were loudly clamoring,
>   >   Demanding to see their mother;

Rich man Wang was
>   On seeing them weeping
>   >   Bereft of courage, fear-stricken.

When he also saw
>   That the sutra chapel
>   >   Was all splattered with blood,

He cried out to Heaven,
>   Overcome by remorse
>   >   More than any man can know.

When all his searches
   Revealed no traces,
      He loudly emitted sad laments,
And leading his children
   He also came looking
      In the flower garden in the back.
When he saw on the wall
   The traces of climbing,
      He knew she had left the house
And he hired people
   To make inquiries
      In all directions, in every place.

Father and children in their anxiety
Shed tears as copiously as a shower,
And Tianlu called out, "My dear father,
Our mother has gone and left us,
So how will we pass our days?
You've got your happy love nest,
But on whom can we two rely?"
And he shouted, "Woman Li,
You forced our mother out of the house!!"

      They searched for her in every direction
      But found no shadow and found no trace.
      Her son and daughter wept day and night;
      Woman Li conceived yet another scheme.

XI. Seeing His Children's Anxiety, the Rich Man Carries a Grudge against Woman Li

[Guojinsuo]
When I remember my dear wife,
My eyes are brimming with tears.
It was you who in the beginning
Came up with that stupid idea yourself!
So I brought home a concubine,
You said to take care of the household
So you could recite "Amitābha"

In order to seek a rebirth in his realm.
Muddled and blinded by drink
I committed oh so many awful deeds.
Because of that damned woman
Suzhen has abandoned the household,
And the sadness of the children
Pierces heart and lungs as with a knife.
Each day I am so disconsolate
That tears course down without pause.

Tell that rich man Wang was anxious for quite a while. Wang Tianlu said to him, "Father, in earlier days when you had not yet married aunt Li and brought her home, we likewise fed monks and handed out donations, but money and goods were still increasing. But since you have married her, you only believe her words. You beat up and cursed out our mother in a hundred ways and even ripped out her left eye. My sister and I were sleeping, but even when you had beaten our mother to death, you should have allowed us to see the corpse, so we could find peace. When we don't see our mother's face, my sister and I can only hang ourselves from a beam and commit suicide to seek death, so all your efforts will have been without result."

When the rich man heard this, a knife pierced his heart and his lungs;
Stamping his feet and beating his breast he emitted loud lamentations.

Tell that the rich man
   Held the hands of his son,
      "You pierce your dad's heart and lungs!
My heart is filled
   With remorse without end,
      As only I myself can know in full."
He also cried out,
   "You cruel wife,
      I am the one who carries the blame,
But how could you leave
   And completely abandon
      These two children, our boy and girl?
Now you have left
   How can I bear
      The loud clamoring of the two children?

You do not know
    That I rather would die—
        Then I would be finished with this all."
When he saw the children
    He involuntarily felt
        As if his heart was smothered with knives,
He sought everywhere,
    But after tens of days
        He found no shadow, he found no trace.
He said, "Dear children,
    Your father committed
        Many heinous and terrible things,
But with your father
    Keeping you company
        You should feel somewhat less sad,
But my son, if you
    Would go on
        And put too much pressure on me,
We can only together
    Butt into each other,
        And all effort will be without result.
As for me
    My remorse
        Is truly unlimited and unbearable,
But you still all day
    Clamor and shout,
        Wanting to see your dear mother!"

Filled with anxiety, the rich man was
Bereft of courage and fear-stricken.
"My dear wife has left without leaving a trace.
She has abandoned our dear children,
On whom are the two of them to rely?
But then those outstanding accounts—
Now the tenth month is approaching
I very much want to collect the cash,
But how can I leave these dear children alone?"

        He kindly stroked his dear child,
            "Please don't be so deeply hurt!

Your father made quite a mistake,
Now pass your days in good cheer."

XII. The Rich Man Thinks about Collecting His Accounts and at the Same Time Searching for Zhang Suzhen

[Guazhixiang]
Silently he heaved a heavy sigh,
Tears coursed down without end.
"These last few days the children have been so sad
That I cannot help myself from feeling heavy at heart.
I am really caught between two demands,
I am really caught between two demands.
We searched for her but no result;
Because of the wine I was wrong.
If only my wife would return to her old home,
I will hold masses
To thank Heaven,
To thank Heaven."

Tell that when rich man Wang had given in to his anxiety for a while, he told woman Li, "These two children are clamoring and howling each day, demanding their mother, but we have conducted searches in all four directions and we have found no information. This endless crying and weeping cannot but fill my heart with pain. Now you here at home will take good care of the children, and I will leave, first of all to collect those accounts, and secondly to search for Suzhen." Woman Li replied, "Husband, you are right. The children are distressed, and I too feel the pain. I'm afraid that she will be staying with some relatives. When you have found her, I will hand her the boy and his sister, so you don't need to worry." When the rich man heard this, sad tears coursed down. He then said to Wang Tianlu, "You should not hang around here at home, but go to school and devote yourself to your studies and be less anxious." And he said to his daughter Huixiang, "You should learn some needlework with your aunt woman Li. That is your task. I will go and search for your mother." When Wang Tianlu heard this, he said, "Father, come home as early as possible whether or not you have news about our mother."

When the rich man heard this, tears coursed down his face,
"My dear son, please don't be so sad while staying at home."

The old rich man
   Was even more anxious
      As he gave his son his instructions,
While Wang Tianlu
   Implored his father
      To come home as soon as possible.
He cried out, "My son!"
   He cried out, "My daughter,
      There is no need to see me off today.
Now I take my leave
   I also do not know
      When we will see each other again."
When rich man Wang
   Had mounted his horse
      And set off on his wide wanderings,
His two children
   Returned to the house,
      Weeping and howling and hollering.
When in the sutra chapel
   They didn't see the mother
      Who had born the two of them,
The tears in their eyes
   Gushed forth like a spring—
      Their weeping almost killed them.
They called out,
   "Cruel mother,
      You abandoned the two of us,
And when you left,
   You didn't even
      Say a single word to us two.
If you had told us
   Only very briefly
      In which region you would settle,
The two of us
   Here back at home
      Could set our worries aside."

Still filled with great anxiety
He said to the girl, "Listen,
I go to the southern school,

While you will stay at home.
Please try to be not too sad."
Both the boy and his sister
Profusely shed many tears,
"Our mother has departed,
When will she be able to return?"

> Tianlu left for the southern school,
> His sister Huixiang felt quite sad.
> Their father left to find their mother,
> When would he be able to return?

XIII. Wang Tianlu Has Left for School, and Suzhen Is Anxiously Traveling On

[Lanhua Ganzhou]
I shiver in the cold wind that pierces me to the bone;
I have barely left hearth and home,
And it is truly unbearable.
When I remember my children, my tears gush down,
They are still so young—who will take care of them?
I have no one to turn to—to whom can I complain?
My heart is depressed
And I pray to Heaven—
I don't know the wrongs I committed in past existences.
All my self-cultivation
Has turned to naught:
Having lost one eye,
My body isn't whole.
My body isn't whole!

Now tell that Zhang Suzhen after leaving home had traveled on for full three days on the road. Going forward she arrived deep in the mountains in an open field at a nunnery that was called Guanyin Dhyana Convent. It was inhabited by nuns who elsewhere had studied seated mediation. Strictly disciplined in body and mind, they fully understood the Three Teachings and securely grasped the text of the sutras. When Suzhen learned that this was a convent of nuns, she wept and collapsed in front of the gate building. The nun in change of affairs came up to her and asked her, "Dear Lady, where are you from? How did you end up in these terrible circumstances?" Suzhen thereupon told the master, "My family lives in Biancheng, in Sanxian Village, also known as Bali Hamlet." When the nun heard this, she promptly said, "Lady, in that village there lives a rich man Wang Zhongqing, and his wife is called Zhang Suzhen. They are famous. I've heard that she understands the Dharma of the Buddha, is well acquainted with principle and nature, clearly grasps inside and outside, and feeds monks and hands out donations, widely creating good karma without any stinginess. Here in this convent are fifty-three nuns who want to go to that place, first of all to greet her, and secondly to beg for a donation of grain for the use of the permanent inhabitants."

>When Suzhen had heard the question of the nun,
>Tears coursed down from her eyes, which filled up.

"Dear old master,
>I am no one else
>>But the wife of that Wang Zhongqing,
That Zhang Suzhen,
>Who feasted the monks
>>And widely handed out rich donations.
When I want to tell
>All of my sufferings,
>>There's no way to tell them completely:
All my fasting
>And Buddha-recitation
>>Were wasted efforts without any result.
I urged my husband,
>The rich man, to marry
>>Woman Li and to make her his wife,
And the family wealth
>I entrusted to her,
>>So I could study religion, undisturbed.
She enticed
>The rich man
>>To administer a beating to my body.
And when one day
>He could not beat me,
>>He became filled with a furious rage.
I was unprepared
>When out of the blue
>>He then ripped out one of my eyes,

Which caused such pain
    That it was unbearable
        And I wept till the night's third watch.
I dreamed that a god
    Then healed my eye,
        Putting a stop to that terrible pain,
And I abandoned
    My son and daughter,
        To make my escape from that house.
In the three days since
    I have left my home,
        I haven't had even one kernel of rice;
And I suffer for my son,
    And I suffer for my daughter—
        On whom will they be able to rely?"

When the nun had heard her story,
She invited her inside the nunnery,
Where she bowed to all the resident nuns,
"Allow me to shave off my hair
And practice self-cultivation here."
When the nuns heard this request,
They strongly advised against it,
"We will hire a number of people
Who can take you back to your own home."

        Suzhen then secretly thought to herself,
         "I am like a bird escaped from the cage:
        Having jumped out of the net of Heaven,
        How would I reenter into that pit of fire?"

XIV. Zhang Suzhen Enters the Nunnery, Shaves Off Her Hair, Leaves the Household, and Practices Self-Cultivation

[Shanpoyang]

I have burst free from the realm of red dust,
But still my heart harbors certain attachments.
The first of these is my fear of life and death;
The second is that I may have escaped from the debts of karmic enemies,

But still I am deeply pained
As they weigh on my breast,
And I blame my husband for lacking in foresight,
Forcing me to leave the family
And living now far from home.
The third is that I cannot let go of my two babies.
Involuntarily tears fill my cheeks,
Heart-broken.
Those several beatings
Forced me to go away.
I've cut my hair and practice self-cultivation,
My single heart free from any blockage or hindrance,
Free from all blockage or hindrance.

Tell that Zhang Suzhen had been anxious for quite a while, but now on the spot shaved off her hair, left the household, and became a nun—but no more about that.

Now tell that rich man Wang had been searching all over the place for Suzhen, but there was no news about her. When he went on to the Eastern Capital, Biancheng, the capital of the state of Liang, he by accident ran into a number of rich men who wanted to go to Hangzhou, first of all for the scenery, but also for conducting some business. When these other rich men saw that rich man Wang looked worried and that he felt no joy, they said to him, "Whenever you came, there was banter and there was laughter. But now you come this time, you look worried—why don't you feel joy?" Rich man Wang then told them, "Friends, you have to know that some days ago when I had had so much drink that I was absolutely drunk, I gave my wife Suzhen two beatings in a single day and also ripped out one of her eyes, so she ran away that night, no one knows where. The two children have been clamoring and howling each day since, and from early morning till late at night their bitter weeping never stops as they demand their mother. Involuntarily my heart feels like it is smothered by knives. Today I left the house to find some distraction." The other rich men said, "We all are going to Hangzhou, first of all for some trade, and secondly for some fun without any hassle."

> When the rich man had heard this, he secretly heaved a sigh,
> And told his friends his vexations compounded by vexations.

He told these men,
  "My dear friends,
    Let me first go back to my house

To instruct my wife,
    Talk to the children,
        And get some white silver together.
Let me buy some safflower
    As well as purpleroot,
        Silks and satins, gauze and woolens.
When I will have told her
    That I will be traveling,
        My wife also has no need to worry."
But the other rich men
    Said with one voice,
        "There is no need to go back home.
Once you are at home,
    You dote on your children
        And cannot succeed in going out.
We all together
    Will give you some money
        That you can pay when we return.
This day is lucky,
    So get all your stuff,
        So we can set out on our journey."
On hearing this,
    The rich man wept
        Tears that sprang from his heart,
"My dear friends,
    Your concern for me
        I will never be able to forget.
So let me now
    Write a letter
        To be delivered to my house,
In which I implore
    My current bed-partner
        To take good care of the children."
When the letter was written
    He kindly asked someone
        To deliver it to his village house,
Because he, rich man Wang,
    And his travel companions
        Could not afford to wait any longer.

"This very day I
   Depart for Hangzhou,
      Please don't indulge in vexations.
My only worry is
   My son and daughter—
      On whom can the two of them rely?"

The rich man was worried
And, deeply moved, sighed,
When would he now be able to return?
"My children will each day
Both profusely shed tears,
And longing for their mother,
And longing for their father.
I have a mind to go home,
But my friends refuse to let me go."

> The rich man was making a journey,
> Straightaway in one go to Hangzhou.
> Painful tears flowed from his eyes
> As he was longing for his children.

XV. After Wang Zhongqing Had Left, the Letter Was Delivered to Woman Li

[Zaoluopao]
When woman Li had carefully read that letter,
Big tears poured down from her brimming eyes.
"After Suzhen had disappeared without a trace,
I thought we two could become a happy couple.
But those children kept clamoring
And didn't overcome their sadness.
On seeing them my husband would burst into tears
And weep all day.
I will force them out of the house,
Force them away!"

Tell that after woman Li had wept, she thought to herself, "Now my husband has left, nothing stands in my way. Wang Tianlu has gone to his school, so let me kill these two little bastards one by one." Women Li then called the girl

Huixiang to her room, and the girl asked, "Mother, what do you want me to do?" Woman Li replied, "Rotten little cheap slut, I told you a moment ago to bring me some water for washing my face. I had taken off my pair of golden-thread chain bracelets and also four silver rings. I had just taken them off, but in the blink of an eye they have disappeared. You little thief, when I saw that you were still so young and your mother had run off, you looked so miserable to me, so pitiable, a child without any champion!" The girl replied, "I never saw those armbands and rings!"

> When woman Li heard this, she exploded in rage,
> And she cursed her out as a slave again and again.

Once woman Li
   Heard her say this,
      Her heart exploded in rage,
And she cried,
   "You little slut,
      You are too brazen and tricky!
In my bedroom
   Has not been
      Any other outside person at all,
So, little slave,
   If it wasn't you,
      Which one could it have been?
I cannot but
   Demand these
      Golden armbands back from you!"
When Huixiang
   Heard her say this,
      It scared her out of her wits,
"Dear mother,
   Don't be so mad
      Because I didn't see them,
So if you now
   Beat me to death,
      I would die without cause."
But woman Li said,
   "If I would now
      Not administer you a beating,

You would, without loot
  And without any tears,
    Refuse to make a confession."
She stripped the child
  Of all the clothes
    She was wearing on her body,
And tied her to
  A low narrow bench
    To give her a cruel beating.
As she grabbed
  A sturdy horsewhip,
    The girl addressed her thusly,
"Dear mother,
  Please take pity
    And spare my miserable life,
Even if you would
  Kill me with a knife,
    I don't know where they are."
But when woman Li
  Heard her say this,
    She only grew more angered,
And she whipped her
  Tens and tens of times:
    Innumerable bloody wounds
From the top of her head
  All the way down to
    Her legs, her shins, her heels!
As she was whipping
  That Wang Tianlu
    Happened to come from school,
And when he saw her
  Beating Huixiang,
    He was scared out of his mind.
He immediately
  Pulled her back,
    That auntie, that woman Li,
And hastily knelt down
  On both his knees,
    As tears poured down his face.

"Dear mother,
   Please take pity
      On the two of us, orphans.
If you beat us
   You'll have others
      Say that you lack all virtue!"
Unable to rouse her,
   He stretched himself out
      On top of his sister's body,
And called, "Mother,
   Rather beat me,
      I will not hate you for that.
When I see that my sister's
   Body has been beaten
      So it is blue and bruised all over,
I feel as if pointed knives
   Are cutting out my heart!"
      And as his tears gushed down,
His sister Huixiang
   Prayed, "Mother,
      Rather give me that beating.
Because if you whip
   My elder brother,
      He cannot pursue his studies."

Elder brother and younger sister,
Bereft of courage, fear-stricken,
Secretly remembered their own mother,
"If our mother were still around,
She would take care of her kids.
She made the wrong decision
By abandoning us as orphans.
Now our father has also left,
And we don't know when he'll return."

      As the children wept, woman Li
      Secretly reached the conclusion:
      "If I whip both of them together,
      It will save me quite some rage."

XVI. Woman Li without Reason Administers a Beating to Wang Tianlu and His Sister Huixiang; Bitterly Suffering, They Are Overcome by Vexation

[Jishengcao]
I'll get you, these criminal lowlifes,
Don't play your tricks on me!
Those golden armbands once put off were gone without a trace—
Slave, you stole them but still refuse to confess!
Handing out my own punishment, there's no pardon
As long as you won't
Deliver your lousy life to me,
Deliver your lousy life to me!

Tell that that woman Li, having said this, thought to herself, "If I whip that wench, that little guy will hold me back, so let me evenly divide this whipping over you two." And she said to Tianlu, "Come to think of it, your sister Huixiang definitely must have stolen those golden armbands and rings for you, so now she refuses to return them to me. Before you had arrived, I had made a vow that I would give your sister a hundred lashes. Now you tell me to beat you, and she tells me to beat her, and the two of you are competing to endure these lashes. I will divide them evenly between the two of you. If the two of you stretch out on a bench, I will give each of you fifty lashes, and then I will not demand these armbands and rings from you anymore. But if you roll away only once from these fifty lashes, it will not count, and I will start all over."

When Wang Tianlu heard this, his face lost all color;
When his sister learned this, her souls fled her body.

Wang Tianlu
   And Huixiang
      Both knelt down together,
Praying, "Mother,
   Please show mercy
      And spare our doomed lives.
If we would steal
   Your gold armbands,
      Of what use would they be?
But still you cruelly
   Beat my little sister
      Without any sign of feeling!

Display some grace
　　For this one time
　　　　And forgive us our faults—
How could you
　　Be so cruel at heart
　　　　And refuse to spare our lives?
If the two of us
　　Beseech you so humbly
　　　　And in such a piteous manner,
How can you,
　　Despite an iron heart,
　　　　Not soften at least a little bit?"
When woman Li
　　Heard his plaint,
　　　　She sneeringly smiled at him,
"Now if you manage
　　To talk me around,
　　　　I'll consider you quite capable."
Then she shouted,
　　"Hurry up and fast!
　　　　Now take off all your clothes,
And if you say
　　One single 'No,'
　　　　Your life won't be spared at all."
While Wang Tianlu
　　Slowly, so slowly
　　　　Took off the clothes he wore,
He longed in his heart
　　For his dear father
　　　　He didn't see come back home,
"If you arrive early,
　　We, father and son,
　　　　Will still be able to see each other,
But in case
　　You arrive late,
　　　　I will likely have lost my life!"
That woman Li
　　Grabbed the horsewhip,
　　　　Lashing him without restraint,

And below the lashes
> His tender skin
>> Was covered in streams of blood.

When cruel-hearted
> She had given them
>> The full number of fifty lashes,

She left the children,
> Overcome by pain,
>> Bitterly crying out their grief,

As they were rolling
> All over the ground,
>> Completely covered in blood,

And Huixiang
> Supported her brother,
>> Bereft of courage, fear-stricken.

That woman Li shouted,
"You two rotten thieves,
There is no need to feel so terrible.
When I see your vexations,
I also feel pain in my heart.
As mother I'll show mercy
And spare your rotten lives,
Seeing that the two of you
Are so fully devoted to your parents."

> That women Li addressed them thusly,
> "Now please listen to my explanation:
> I treat the two of you extremely well,
> But you will not treat me as parent."

XVII. After Woman Li upon Administering a Beating Has Returned to Her Room, Huixiang Supports Wang Tianlu

[Shanpoyang]
Wang Tianlu had been left utterly unconscious
And Huixiang supported him with both bands.
"My situation is so painful it's hard to endure!

The mother who bore me, where may she be?
I also have no father,
Don't see him return.
We encounter today
Trials and torments:
We are cursed out, beaten up, submitted to torture!
I resent, how I resent
That wolf-hearted father
Who is doting on that no-good woman Li.
How sad,
We brother and sister almost lost our lives!
How sad,
My whole body aches, I can't move a step!"

Tell that Huixiang supported her brother Wang Tianlu with both her hands. After they had given in to their vexations for quite a while, they returned to their rooms—and no more about that.

Now tell that woman Li thought to herself, "If I give them a beating each day, I am wasting my energy, and I will have the neighbors say that I am no good. When I will now send Wang Tianlu off to his school, I will first kill this wench and then kill that boy. That should be easy." As soon as she had said so, she went over to the western house, and she called Wang Tianlu, "In her rage your mother has yesterday given you some lashes, so now I am filled with unbearable remorse. You should go to your school to study. How come you haven't yet left? When your father comes home, he'll berate me, won't he?" When Wang Tianlu heard this, he left for school despite the pain.

Now tell that woman Li in deepest secret bought some poison, and put it in a bowl of noodle soup. "If I let that child eat this, she'll die by herself, and he will have no cause to carry a grudge." She had prepared everything in all details—but no more about that.

Now tell that Wang Tianlu returned from his school. When woman Li saw that he had come home, she lay down on her bed and claimed that she was not feeling well. Tianlu and Huixiang promptly asked, "Mother, what is wrong with you?" Woman Li replied, "Children, I thought that you these last few days hadn't had any delicious meal, so I prepared some sesame seed noodles. They are there in the wok. But because I am suddenly not feeling well, the two of you should go ahead and have some. Don't let them go sour." When Wang Tianlu heard his, he hastily filled a bowl of hot soup and offered it to woman

Li. Woman Li didn't say a word, but thought to herself, "I wanted this child to eat it and die, but now he has me eat from it first." So she said, "My child, I'm too sick to eat anything. You two should eat some." But Tianlu on hearing this replied, "Mother, if you will not eat, we wouldn't dare do so. You should first have a mouthful of this hot soup, and then afterwards we will have some." Woman Li pushed the bowl toward Wang Tianlu, and he pushed it toward her, but when by accident he spilled half of the soup on the ground, flames rose three feet high!

> Spilling the soup, it falls on the dust of the floor:
> Flames rise up that reach a height of three feet.

As soon as Tianlu,
    Saw this sight,
        His heart was scared, his gall aflutter,
While Huixiang
    Was holding back
        Her brother, born of one mother.
Brother and sister
    Loudly wept,
        Shouting at the top of their voices,
"If this stuff
    Would reach our stomach,
        Flesh would have turned into pus!
But it must be
    That the two of us
        Are not yet destined to die—
We pray the gods
    To take pity on us,
        Little children without a champion!
Now in the case
    Something would
        Have happened to the two of us,
Our father and mother
    On coming home,
        Would only grasp an empty void."
And they cried out,
    "You cruel father,
        You didn't think things through:

Whether you found her,
    Or whether you didn't,
        You should have quickly returned."
Now when woman Li
    Saw them weeping,
        She quickly decided on a scheme,
And she cursed them,
    "You little bastards,
        How brazen you are, how cunning!
When I yesterday,
    Rightly or wrongly,
        Administered you a light beating,
You deviously
    Bought some poison
        In order to murder your mother!"
In greatest hurry
    She called together
        The neighbors on both sides,
And this woman Li
    Laid out in detail
        Her accusation quite clearly.

"A few days ago this little slave
Had stolen my golden armbands,
But upon questioning she did not confess.
So I gave the girl some lashes,
And then I let the matter rest.
But who could have thought
They would hatch a scheme
And get this poison to use it?
May dragons and devas watch from above!

        "My dear neighbors, you are my witnesses,
        The dragons and gods aborted their plans.
        Those bastards wanted to cause my death,
        But I thank my life to these guardian gods."

XVIII. Woman Li Wants to Send Them to Court, but Afraid the Case Will Not Stand Up to Scrutiny, She Administers to Both of Them Twenty Strokes of the Big Cudgel

[Zaoluopao]

Holding the cudgel in her hands,
Gnashing her teeth, determined,
She loudly cursed out the two children,
"At this young age, still so little,
You're lacking all human feeling:
You put in the poison to destroy my life!
Now the neighbors urge mercy,
I would rather not follow them,
But then the people would say
I have no love or affection for these brats.
But twenty strokes
Cannot untie the hatred in my breast!"

[Zaoluopao]

The two children wept:
Their skin broken, their flesh bruised;
As the red blood flowed,
Their tears profusely coursed down.
"To whom can we tell the wrong we have suffered?
We may have a mouth, but there's no one to listen;
Our father has left and we don't see him come back.
Our lives are bound before long
To leave for the Yellow Springs.[16]
Longing for our parents
We weep till our liver and innards break,
Liver and innards break."

Tell that woman Li, because of the intercession of the neighbors, administered the two children a beating of twenty strokes with the heavy cudgel. Woman Li also told Wang Tianlu, "The two of you should not go back to the western house. I am not feeling well, so you should sleep at the back gate, and Huixiang has to sleep in front, so don't go over there." Wang Tianlu replied, "Mother, of course." Put aside the two children and don't talk about them.

---

16. "Yellow Springs" is a common designation for the underworld.

Now tell that woman Li thought to herself, "Tonight I am going to kill those two bastards. Then I will throw open the gate, screaming at the top of my voice. I will say that I am chasing robbers away, and once I have awakened the neighbors on both sides, claim they were killed by bandits, so no blame will be attached to me." When woman Li had come up with this idea, she sharpened a knife. Seeing that it was still quite early and not yet the time to take action, she went to sleep for a while, so she would be ready to kill those bastards. As soon as woman Li had fallen asleep, the gods picked up sleep-bugs and placed them on her body, so she snored like the thunder. Then the gods shouted at the top of their voices, "Tianlu, don't feign to be asleep. Tonight your aunt wants to kill the two of you, so you have to flee now." Tianlu woke up with a start. Greatly scared, he hurried to the rear room, and by the light of the lamp he saw clearly the steel knife by the side of woman Li. With tears coursing down from his eyes, he ran to the front gate, and shouted, "Quickly get up! Our aunt wants to kill the two of us, so we have to flee for our lives right now."

After Wang Tianlu had shouted this three times,
He forgot about his little sister and ran for his life.

Wang Tianlu
   Warned his sister
      To run away and flee for her life,
So Huixiang
   All of a sudden
      Suffered quite a frightening scare.
When she rose up,
   She ran after him
      Out through the gate in the back,
While she shouted,
   "You cruel brother!"
      Lamenting at the top of her voice.
"For what reason
   Have you forgotten about me?
      Where have you hidden yourself?
Loudly weeping
   She only caught up with him
      In the flower garden in the back.
When Tianlu heard
   His sister's voice,
      His heart felt smothered by knives,

And below the high wall
   He lowered his voice
      To address his sister of one mother,
Saying, "Dear sister,
   Don't be so upset,
      We now have to flee for our lives.
But I was afraid
   That I might wake up
      That no-good person woman Li."
Brother and sister
   Saw the wall was too high
      For them to make their escape,
"When all too soon
   Dawn will break,
      How will we be able to flee?"
He first supported
   His sister Huixiang
      To climb across that high wall,
Then Wang Tianlu
   With the help of the gods
      Also escaped from the garden.
On the one hand weeping,
   On the other hand running,
      They turned around to look,
"Today we too
   Abandon our home—
      When will we be able to return?
We also don't know
   When our father and mother
      Will arrive here in this place,
But once back home
   They will look for us,
      Weeping will kill our parents."

While on the road brother and sister
Painfully wept, overcome by grief,
As they hurried onward without ever resting.
"Now today we have left our house,
Who will be our father and mother?"
As Wang Tianlu grasped the hand

Of his full sister born to one mother,
They only feared to be overtaken,
So they went on forward that very moment.

> They wept in a quite unbearable way
> At the fork in the road at Shuangyang:
> One branch went off to the northeast,
> The other went off to the northwest.

XIX. When Wang Tianlu Arrives at the Fork in the Road at Shuangyang, Brother and Sister Each Go Their Own Way

[Miandaxu]

The sky was dark, the earth was black, as the road came to an end:
One branch went to the northwest,
And another went off to the northeast.
How saddening!
They thought of both their parents,
"You have abandoned your children,
To whom can we now go and appeal?
We have barely escaped with our lives.
Having abandoned home and hearth,
We pray to the gods,
We pray to the gods!"

Tell that Wang Tianlu and his sister Huixiang had left their home. After they had walked for quite a while on the road, they came, to their vexation, to the fork in the road in Shuangyang—but no more about that.

Wang Tianlu then said to Huixiang, "The roosters are crowing, so I'm afraid it soon will be light. I'm afraid our aunt will send people to track us down and overtake us. As long as we are walking together, it is easy for people to recognize us, and we are easy to find. That's why of the two of us, brother and sister, you must go to the northeast while I will go to the northwest, so each of us can escape with his life." When Huixiang heard this, tears gushed forth like a spring, and she said, "Brother, you are afraid that I will be a burden to you, and that's why you want to part from me. But to whom should I appeal? Let's seek death, and die in one spot. How can you cruelly bear to abandon me, to leave me behind?" When they had spoken, they wept at the top of their voices.

> When Tianlu heard her say this, tears poured from his eyes;
> He held the hand of his little sister as he voiced sad laments.

"Dear little sister,
   I am not afraid
      That you will be a burden to me,
But I only say
   That walking together
      We will not be able to escape.
If we two
   Separate
      And each seek their own way,
We will eventually,
   If we survive,
      Be able to see each other again.
If we stay together
   And back at home
      They have people come after us,
They will take back
   The two of us,
      And we are sure to lose our lives.
I have here
   This handkerchief
      That I will give to you as a token.
If you, sister,
   Take this handkerchief,
      It may later serve as a proof."
His sister Huixiang
   Stretched out her hand
      To accept that handkerchief,
While from her eyes
   Tears streamed down—
      Bereft of courage, fear-stricken.
"My dear brother,
   I would rather
      Seek death and not separate,
Because if by chance
   Something would happen,
      All our effort would be in vain."
Having said this,
   She loudly wept,
      And knelt down on both knees,

"When you have found
    A safe place to stay,
        Please do not worry too much;
Once at your place,
    Inquire about me,
        Gather information in all places;
If I by any chance
    Find a good place,
        I will make inquiries about you."
Wang Tianlu
    Told his sister,
        "Don't give in to vexation!
Since ancient times
    Fear of separation
        Has ruined many a career!"
Brother and sister,
    Going their own ways,
        Wept at the top of their voices.
Wang Tianlu
    Strode off
        And went on ahead on his way,
"I only resent
    My father
        For lacking all determination,
Letting woman Li
    Rip apart and disperse
        That whole family of ours!"
His sister Huixiang
    Went to the northeast,
        Crying at the top of her voice,
"Now my brother
    Has said goodbye,
        When will I ever see him again?"

The two of them, brother and sister,
Traveled along their separate ways.
Now narrate how that no-good person woman Li
Suddenly woke up from her sleep,
Startled awake she was frightened.
Grabbing her knife, she ran straight

To the rear gate of the house, and
When she didn't find that bastard,
She turned around and went to the front gate.

> When she searched at the front gate,
> She also did not find that little slave.
> The bastards were not bound to die,
> They're assisted by ghost and gods.

XX. When Woman Li Goes Looking for the Two Children, They Have Left without a Trace

[Zaoluopao]

Of Wang Tianlu
There was no word, there was no news;
And of Huixiang
There was no trace, there was no sign.
She carefully searched the front part and the back part of the house,
She made inquiries with the neighbors to the east and to the west.
She sent people out to overtake them,
She made inquiries with all relatives.
These two bastards had mysteriously
Disappeared from the family mansion.
"Come to think of it,
I involuntarily feel quite depressed,
Feel quite depressed."

Tell that woman Li searched for the two children, but they had disappeared without any trace—no more about that.

Now tell that Wang Tianlu was twelve years old, but Huixiang was only nine. Having left house and home, she felt lonely and utterly disconsolate. Now she thought of her parents of whom she did not know where they were, then she worried about where her brother might end up. For three full days she walked on. Everybody loved her and each family wanted to keep her, but this child had no intention to stay. Going forward she arrived at the gate of a convent, so Huixiang asked the masters, "What kind of place is this?" They replied, "This is called the Guanyin Dhyana-Grove Convent; it's only nuns who live here." This child wept and cried, cried and wept there in front of the gate. She would like to go inside, but she saw some big dogs lying there and obstructing the gate. Lowering her head, she sighed, "Dear mother who bore me, where may you be right now? Our father has gone without any news, and where may my brother have settled? How can you know the many miseries I have suffered out on the road?" After a sigh, she wept at the top of her voice. One nun, who right that moment was burning incense in the Devaraja Hall, suddenly heard this child weeping in a heart-breaking way, and when she hastily came out of the gate to have a look, she saw this adorable little girl weeping there. This nun went to the Dhyana Hall and said, "Abbess Suzhen, in front of the gate there is this little girl that is weeping, and with every word she says that her suffering is killing her, so let's go and have a look."

When Suzhen heard this, she went with the other nuns to the temple gate. It was dusk, and when Suzhen saw this child, she promptly thought of her own children, and she felt as if her heart was smothered by knives while tears gushed down. She stepped forward and asked the little girl, "Where are you from? And what is your name? Are your parents still alive? And why did you leave house and home? Please tell me everything from the beginning."

> When she heard these questions, she felt as if smothered by knives;
> Overcome by anxiety she told them about her home and her family.

"Dear masters,
   My family is
      From the Eastern Capital Bianliang;
In Bali Hamlet,
   That is Sanxian Village,
      There stands the house of our family.
My father is
   Wang Zhongqing,
      Who has a family capital of millions;
My mother is
   Zhang Suzhen
      Who loves to read the holy sutras.
She urged
   My father
      To marry a certain woman Li,
Thinking that she
   Instead of my mother
      Would take care of household affairs.
But that no-good woman
   Convinced my father
      By her sweet words and little lies

That he shouldn't let
   My dear mother
      Make donations and feed monks.
She inveigled my father
   To administer beatings
      To the mother who gave me life,
But my mother
   Insisted on feeding monks
      Without feeling any regret at all.
Then one day
   When my father
      Came home as drunk as could be,
That woman Li
   By her false words
      Made him mad at my mother
And he ripped out
   My mother's
      Left eye.
Our dear mother
   Abandoned us
      And left without leaving a trace.
We clamored
   To our dear father,
      Demanding to see our mother,
And then our father
   Abandoned us—
      We haven't seen him return.
Now this woman Li
   Bitterly abused us
      In a hundred of kinds of ways;
She also used poison
   But that was exposed
      Thanks to a move of her son.
Then late at night
   She got out a knife,
      Intending to kill both of us,
But thanks to the gods
   Who warned us in time
      We escaped from the house.

When we arrived
   At the Shuangyang fork,
      We were long in a quandary,
But my elder brother
   Feared people were following,
      So we then there parted our ways.
My dear brother
   Went to the northwest,
      Weeping as he pursued his road,
And I arrived,
   Weeping my way,
      Here after three full days."[17]
When Zhang Suzhen
   Had heard this tale,
      Her heart was smothered by knives
And with both arms
   She embraced the child,
      Bereft of courage, fear-stricken.
She said, "My child,
   I am none other than
      The mother who bore you.
I have wept until
   My liver and innards broke
      Out of longing for my children.
Fortunately you,
   Your brother and you,
      Could both escape with your lives,
But for what reason,
   And in what manner,
      Could you end up so far apart?
My darling son,
   In which place
      May you end up on this journey?
In vain was my piety
   Because my whole family,
      Has been completely dispersed!"

---

17. Throughout this scene Huixiang will be kneeling with her face to the ground.

In her anxiety Suzhen
Prayed to the deities,
"Protect the one still out on the road.
If my son and daughter
Can be reunited again,
I will sponsor masses
To thank all the gods.
The present sufferings
Are all caused by our former lives."

> When mother and daughter had cried
> She retained the girl in the nunnery.
> She lit incense and constantly prayed
> For the protection of her dear son.

XXI. Huixiang Is Retained in the Convent and Wang Tianlu Arrives at the King Guan Temple at Tong Pass

[Zaoluopao]

He asked for tea and begged for food
On both the main streets and markets.
When evening fell, he sought shelter in a temple hall—
In his anxiety he prayed to King Guan,[18]
"You are the loyal general of a former dynasty.
How can I bear my present sufferings and tribulations?
Please take pity on me, one
Who's left home and hearth.
I pray you, dear god,
To protect me against disasters!"

[Zaoluopao]

King Guan displayed his power and godly descended
When he saw the child weep in this heart-rending way.
"At present the Golden Troops rebel out in the west,[19]

---

18. King Guan is the deified Guan Yu (d. 219), who from the Song dynasty onward was widely venerated as a god of war and a god of riches. See Haar 2017.
19. This is a puzzling line. The "Golden Troops" most likely refer to the armies of the Jürched Jin (Gold) dynasty, which was established in 1115 in present-day northeast China and conquered northern China up to the Huai in 1126 and the following years. The Tong Pass, on the border of Henan and

The court is bound to make good use of this person."
King Guan thereupon called,
"Little boy who are still so young,
Practice civil and martial arts in your dream!"
He awoke with a start from a Southern Bough dream,
A Southern Bough dream.

Tell that King Guan instructed Wang Tianlu throughout the night in the nine military arts on the left side and the nine military arts on the right side, in all eighteen military arts of both the left and the right side, until he was perfectly skilled in each and every one. "I also dreamed that I swallowed both the sun and the moon, and that my eyes devoured several celestial books in three scrolls and divine texts on the Six Scales,[20] and that I further ate two dough tigers and nine dough oxen." On waking up, he had the strength of nine oxen and two tigers, and waited for the arrival of dawn.

At Tong Pass there was an assistant regional commander, Li Yong, who, as ordered by a sage edict from the imperial court, opened the exercise grounds, hiring troops and selecting officers. When Wang Tianlu had entered the exercise grounds and greeted assistant regional commander Li Yong, he demonstrated his skills with the one-sided knife, the two-sided sword, the three-pronged fork, and the four-sided staff, but these were not counted exceptional. He then also demonstrated his skills with the curved battle-axe, the long lance and the short sword, and the steel whip for beating generals, and when the officers and troops saw Wang Tianlu's daring bravery, all people shouted hurrah. With a broad smile of joy assistant regional commander Li Yong ordered his underling to set up a target at the distance of 360 paces on which a gold coin was hung: Whether he would hit the hole in the coin[21] with all three arrows or only with one, this would be a man to drive back the Golden Troops and defeat the rebel bandits! When Wang Tianlu heard this, he held the bow in his hand, placed the arrow on the string, and hit the target with all three arrows!

Shaanxi, was heavily garrisoned because of its strategic importance but is not a logical place to fight Jin invaders. Shang Lixin (2018, 125) emends 西下返金兵 to 西夏返金兵, which would have to be translated as "The Xixia rebel against the Jin troops," but this makes no sense because Wang Tianlu is said to fight and defeat the Golden Troops in the text below.

20. The Six Scales (*liujia* 六甲) are fearsome warrior gods, "able to move gods and thunders and to subdue demons and gods." If one knows their names and the right formulas to command them and their troops, one can summon them to defeat one's human and divine enemies. Originally they are the gods of the days including the character *jia* in the cycle of sixty days.

21. Traditional Chinese copper coins had a square hole in the middle.

Wang Tianlu hit the target three times in a row,
Filling with joy His Excellency the commander.

He called, "Young man,
   What is your hometown?
      And what the district and prefecture?
How old may you be
   That you have mastered
      The military arts to such perfection?"
Wang Tianlu said,
   "Your Excellency,
      Please listen now I report these facts.
In Bali Village
   Near the city of Bianliang
      One may find the house of our family.
My father is
   Wang Zhongqing,
      And my mother is surnamed Zhang,
But he later
   Also married
      A no-good concubine named Li.
She inveigled
   My dear father
      To administer our mother a beating
Because my mother
   All her life loved
      To feed monks and make donations.
My dear father,
   Because he was drunk,
      Even ripped out one of her eyes.
While my sister and I
   Were fast asleep
      And never woke up for a moment,
Our dear mother
   Abandoned us,
      Leaving for some unknown place,
And when our father
   Searched for her,
      He found neither shadow nor trace.

That woman Li
    By all means
        Bitterly tried to kill the two of us,
But thanks to the gods
    We were warned
        And could escape from the house.
When the two of us
    Traveling arrived at
        The fork in the road at Shuangyang,
We wept quite long
    But with no destination
        We there decided to part our ways.
My little sister
    Wept and went off
        In the northeasterly direction,
While I today,
    Having nowhere to go,
        Have decided to join the army."
Commander Li
    On hearing this tale
        Was moved to sighs without end,
"This whole family
    Has suffered so much
        That the emotion is nearly killing."

After the troops had been hired,
The orders reached the garrison,
And Wang Tianlu set out on campaign.
In each battle he was victorious,
Achieving success upon arrival.
Seeing him, the Golden Troops
To the last man were frightened.
Upon this report the authorities
Informed the Sagely Enlightened Ruler.

> Tianlu achieved numerous victories,
> So the court accepted the proposal:
> Assistant commander Wang Tianlu!
> Li Yong promoted to commander!

XXII. Wang Tianlu Has Obtained the Office of Assistant Regional Commander and Wang Zhongqing Returns Home from Hangzhou

[Shanpoyang]
When I think of the past,
It was I who made the mistake.
On top of that I married
As concubine a no-good slut.
Because of her I was abandoned by my wife
And I was pestered by the clamoring children.
They pained me so much it was unbearable,
As each day they voiced their resentment.
My heart was filled with remorse,
But then I unexpectedly left on this trading trip.
On whom could my two children there rely
After I had abandoned my house and home?
My tears resemble a shuttle.
I enjoy wealth and luxury
And my wife suffers pain.
When I hear that my family is dispersed,
Whom can I blame but myself,
Only myself!

Tell that Wang Zhongqing and the other rich men at Suzhou and Hangzhou had bought and acquired all kinds of sundry goods. After they had rented a boat and loaded it, they chose a date and set out. After they had traveled for several days, they arrived at the Yangzi River. Now it was Heaven's fate that the rich man was bound to suffer deprivation and with his wife would be tormented like this, not protected by dragons and devas. When their boat had raised sail and arrived in the middle of the river, suddenly a freak storm arose that whipped the stream into thousand-tiered waves. After warding these off a few times, the boat was hit and its planks broke: sun and moon were covered by clouds, the precious goods sank into the river, and the merchants all died. Zhongqing grasped a plank of the boat and had almost lost his life.

It turned out that in this freak storm five of the eight rich men had died, and that only Wang Zhongqing and two others had survived, each by clinging to a plank of the boat. When the wind had blown them to the bank of the river and they had clambered out of the water, it took the three rich men quite a while to regain their senses, and they wept at the top of their voices.

> Traveling on, these three men were overcome by vexations,
> Making their way back home by begging from door to door.

While he was walking
 Wang Zhongqing
  Secretly heaved a heavy sigh
When he remembered
 That sutra-reading
  Person who loved pious works.
"I remember how we
 In those past days
  Always enjoyed lucky blessings.
Who could have known
 That I now at present
  Would only escape with my life?
I only thought
 That my wealth and status
  Would last till my dying day,
How did I know
 That I right now
  Would suffer such poverty?
I have a good wife,
 A son and a daughter,
  But how would they know
That I today
 Far from home
  Make a living by begging?
When the moment comes,
 I will be unable to leave
  My last instructions to my son.
Thinking of this
 I am involuntarily
  Bereft of courage, fear-stricken."

As Zhongqing was traveling,
The hunger was unbearable,
[How could he not] heave many a sigh?

"My suffering has no limit,
Making a living by begging.
Who knew that I'd turn into
This one single naked body?
My clothes are all in tatters—
How will I be able to face my relatives?"

> The rich man walked all the way home,
> But who in his family could know this?
> At night he lodged in temple buildings,
> Overcome by vexations shedding tears.

XXIII. Wang Zhongqing Is Overcome by Vexations in a Temple and Heaven Sends Down the Fire Star to Burn His House and Goods

[Huangying'er]
The Jade Emperor had assembled the Three Parties,[22]
"He lacks the blessings to enjoy his gold and silver,
Trusting that damned woman, he let her jump about,
So the blessed one left the house.
How can the Star of Destruction forgive him
For the evil karma he created day after day?
Descend from the misty clouds
And burn his house and goods to ashes.
By only creating this evil karma,
He invited this disaster."

[Huangying'er]
To burn down that no-good woman the celestial fire
Arrived in the mortal world at the hour of midnight.
That rotten slut had not gone to bed and was drinking,
And ordered a maid to snuff the lamp.
The maid bumped into a God of Fire
When fiery flames burst from the stove.
A fierce smoke arose
When the house got on fire,

---

22. The term "Three Parties" refers the accuser, the accused, and the witnesses in a law case. Here it may be understood as "all concerned."

Coloring the whole sky red,
The whole sky red.

Tell that woman Li right at the hour of midnight was in for some fun, when she suddenly saw that flames burst from the stove on three sides. When a frightened woman Li looked up, she saw the fire dancing all over the beams. She also saw that tables and chairs and benches as well as all big and little boxes were one huge fire. This was really a big fire:

> The flames rose as high as ten thousand rods;
> The thousand-tiered fiery flames rose up to the ninth heaven!
> Entering into the earth, they burned and boiled the Yellow Springs;
> The trees in gardens and groves turned to black stumps.
> The grain and rice in the storehouse changed into dirt and dust;
> The gold and silver in the vats melted like ice.
> The fire in the house lasted for ten full days
> But none of the neighbors suffered the slightest harm.

The rich man's house and goods were completely burned down.

Now tell that when woman Li saw that the celestial fire had burned the big house completely to ashes and she had no place to stay, she wept at the top of her voice.

> Stamping her feet and beating her breast she heaved a sigh:
> From this moment on it was clear she would suffer poverty.

Tell that woman Li
   Burst into tears
      That spoke to her issues of concern:
Of all her fine clothes
   She was not wearing
      Even one on her body at the moment.
"How can my man
   Traveling away from home
      Come to know the situation at home,
That we had a fire
   That burned house and goods
      And I now suffer poverty and want?"
The whole night long
   She longed for her husband,
      Shedding tears without interruption,

"I got holes in my eyes
   From watching for him,
      But I still don't see him come home."
While filled with anxiety
   She received a letter
      That had been sent by her husband,
And she went
   To meet her husband
      Halfway on his journey back home.
When she saw him,
   His clothes in tatters,
      His sallowed face lean from hunger,
She held on to him
   And while weeping
      Asked him the following question:
"Engaging in trade
   Far away from home,
      How did you end up in this manner?"
And he replied,
   "We encountered a storm,
      And barely escaped with our lives.
While on the road
   We had no money,
      So begged for food from door to door;
Enduring hunger,
   Suffering misery,
      We had no place where we could stay."
When woman Li heard
   Her husband's story,
      Her heart felt as smothered by knives,
And holding on
   To her husband
      She wailed at the top of her voice.
"After you left
   The two children
      Disappeared without leaving a sign,
We sought everywhere
   For several tens of days,
      But found no shadow, found no trace.

Then celestial fire
   Burned our house and goods
      Completely so nothing was left
And I at present
   At our own house
      Have not even a place to stay."
When the rich man
   Had heard her story,
      His three souls abandoned his body;
He cried out once,
   "This is too much!"
      And then collapsed on the ground.
When after a while
   He came around,
      His lips were black, his mouth purple,
Leaving woman Li
   There at his side
      Completely flurried and flustered.
"Now in case
   Once again
      Something awful happened to you,
You abandon me
   Without any support—
      Would I be able to make a living?"
The old rich man
   All of a sudden
      Thought of woman Zhang, Suzhen,
And was grieved by
   His two children,
      Gone without a shadow or a trace!
He called out, "My son,
   You abandoned me,
      My heart feels as smothered by knives!
How could you
   Be so cruel
      As to abandon your own father?"
His children were gone
   Without leaving news,
      His house and goods were all burned.

When he saw his house,
>   It was burned to the ground:
>>   No roots of the grasses were left.

The rich man and woman Li
Were moved to pained sighs.
The many family members of his clerks
All came and clamored for
The return of their relatives.
"How come you came home
But they didn't make it back?
We will lodge an accusation
And fight this matter out with you in court!"

>   "Well considered this is unbearable—
>   And every family demands their men.
>   The best is to make a clean escape
>   And flee to a place that cannot be found."

XXIV. The Rich Man and Woman Li Hide Themselves in Another District, and Far from Home Ask for Tea and Beg for Food

[Huameixu]
Tears kept pouring from their eyes;
Away from home in strange lands life is hard.
How could they after enjoying luxury and wealth,
How could they endure this hardship?
"Thinking of the children my heart feels as smothered by knives,
I've wept till my liver and innards are broken.
How pitiable!
If I ever can see them again,
I will sponsor masses to thank dragons and devas,
Thank dragons and devas!"

Tell that the rich man and woman Li lived far from home in strange lands. There was no limit to their misery as they asked for food from door to door and made their living by begging—but no more about that.

Now tell that Wang Tianlu had joined assistant regional commander Li Yong in his campaign against the Golden Troops. He was victorious at every stretch and gained the field in every battle; he achieved success on arrival, and completely vanquished the Golden Troops. Assistant regional commander Li Yong knew how courageous Wang Tianlu was, and having only one child, a girl, he gave her to Wang Tianlu as wife.

Now tell that the imperial court appointed assistant regional commander Li Yong as the marshal commander-in-chief for the subjugation of the world, and appointed Wang Tianlu as the commander in charge of the defense of Tong Pass—each man was allowed to return to his hometown in order to sacrifice at the graves and bow to the ancestors. When Wang Tianlu received this imperial edict, he bowed down and performed twenty-four bows in a row, shouting three times, "Ten thousand years! May you at all times be an imperial lord of eternal joy!"

> When Wang Tianlu had bowed to thank for the imperial edict,
> Tears like pearls streamed down from his overflowing eyes.

Now Wang Tianlu
   Suddenly remembered
      The father who had sired him;
As tears streamed from
   His brimming eyes,
      He wept at the top of his voice.
"Having left my home
   I have now at present
      Achieved both glory and status,
But when I think of
   My little sister,
      Thousands of arrows pierce my heart.
Ever since the day
   That, at the fork in the road,
      We brother and sister parted ways,
I have had no clue
   Where she drifted to
      And where she has settled down.
And where did I leave
   The mother who bore me,
      In what place does she live?
If something happened
   To her in strange lands,
      How would I ever get to know?

After taking my leave
  Of my father-in-law,
    Both from him and his spouse,
I will today
  Go back home
    And search out my two parents."
Commander Li Yong
  Dispatched infantry and cavalry
    To escort Tianlu to his home.
The cannon resounded,
  With its three shots
    Shaking heaven and earth.
In front were displayed
  Flags of the five regions,[23]
    Lances, knives, swords, and spears;
One pair of staves,
  One pair of axes,
    And one pair of drawn bows.
The whip-drum resounded,
  The horn was blown,
    The trumpet and other instruments;
There were long lances
  As well as short lances,
    That paired together went in front.
A squadron of cavalry,
  A squadron of infantry,
    Pressing planks[24] and short cudgels,
And two imperial
  Two-sided swords
    That took lives and chased souls.[25]
Servants held
  A yellow gauze parasol
    Above his head for his protection,

---

23. Flags in the colors of the five directions (east, west, north, south, and center).
24. Pressing planks are an instrument of torture used in interrogations.
25. Swords that allowed the bearer to execute death sentences without first reporting to the emperor.

While he was seated
    In an eight-men sedan chair,
        With troops both in front and in back.
Upon arrival at
    The Ten-Mile Pavilion,[26]
        He said goodbye to his father-in-law,
"My dear father,
    Don't be anxious,
        And please set your worries aside."
This Li Yong
    Cried tears of pain
        As he returned, weeping the while,
And Wang Tianlu
    As well as his wife
        Was seated in their sedan chairs.
When on the road
    They had traveled for
        Some ten days or half a month,
He suddenly thought
    Of his dear mother—
        Bereft of all courage, fear-stricken.

As the anxious Wang Tianlu
Heaved a heart-broken sigh,
He prayed to the gods passing overhead,
"If mother and son in the end
May meet each other again,
And the family be reunited,
I'll never forget your favor
And I'll sponsor ceremonies
To express my thanks to all divinities!"

        When he lifted his head and had a look,
        He saw a palace of the Brahma King:[27]
        The buildings had been newly painted,
        And bronze drums resounded in tune.

---

26. The Chinese mile is about one-third of an imperial mile. The Ten-Mile Pavilion is a pavilion outside town for seeing off departing visitors.

27. Brahma King is one of the many titles of the Buddha.

XXV. Wang Tianlu, Not Far from the Convent, Is Welcomed by the Nuns

[Huangying'er]
In the Seventh Month Yulan[28] is celebrated:
Every family makes offerings for their ancestors
And in the convent all are reciting the true sutras.
Right at the hour of noon
The horns blared to the sky,
As the whip-drums boomed.
"We come to the convent
So do not tarry or delay!"
Orderly lined up, the nuns
Welcomed the commander-in-chief.

Tell that the nuns welcomed His Excellency Wang. Kneeling down in a row, they invited him in, "Please visit the convent to come in from the wind and have some tea." When Wang Tianlu heard they were children and grandchildren of pious families,[29] he was quite pleased, and turned his troops toward the convent. After he had paid his respects to the Buddha image, and once they had taken their seats and drunk their tea, Tianlu admired the streamers and banners and precious parasols. The sutra tables were arranged along the two sides, and pious men and devout women filled the steps. When Tianlu had observed this, he asked the nuns, "What is this grand celebration in your convent?" The nuns replied, "Today is the fifteenth day of the Seventh Month, when Mulian saved his mother: the grand Yulanpen festival. The things each individual offers, such as rice, flour, oil, sauce, tea, and fruits, are sent to the storehouse for venerating the Buddha and feeding the nuns. As for their family affairs, each one writes supplications praying for the salvation and deliverance of their parents."

When Tianlu heard this, he thought of the mother who bore him, and of his sister Huixiang, and his heart felt as if smothered by knives as his tears gushed forth. So he told the nuns, "Five years ago my mother left her house and I was separated from my younger sister. I still don't know whether my mother and sister are still alive. Please prepare a request for me: If my mother and sister are still alive, may it increase their blessings and extend their longevity, and if they

---

28. Yulanpen (or the Ghost Festival) is celebrated on the fifteenth day of the seventh month. The festival celebrates how the holy monk Mulian saved his mother from hell. By making offerings to the clergy on this day, one hoped to ensure a speedy and propitious rebirth of deceased relatives. One also made donations to hungry ghosts.
29. Common monks and nuns enjoyed a poor reputation.

have left this world, may it ensure their deliverance and rebirth in heaven." Having said so, he offered ten taels of white silver for use by the resident community. On hearing this, the nuns accepted the donation and said, "Your Excellency, please tell us your place of registration, the names of your father and mother, and the name of your younger sister."

> When Wang Tianlu heard this request of the nuns,
> He was filled by emotion on listing his hometown.

"Dear masters,
   Please write down
      That to the northeast of Bianliang
Sanxian Village,
   That is Bali Hamlet,
      Is the place of my ancestral home.
This filial son
   Wang Tianlu,
      His mind made up, entrusts his fate
To the father of all creatures
   At the thousand-flower terrace,
      The world-honored one Śākyamuni.
I now recommend
   The mother who bore me,
      The woman Zhang, known as Suzhen,
And I too recommend
   My sister Huixiang,
      Who was born with me of one mother:
If mother and daughter
   Are still in this world, may He
      Increase their blessing, and longevity,
And if they left this world,
   May He save them from hell
      To let them be reborn in a good place."
When he had said this,
   This High Lordship
      Wept in an uncontrollable manner,
Overcome by anxiety,
   So a young nun
      Handed him a fresh cup of tea.

Over her shoulder
   She wore a handkerchief
      Which Tianlu happened to see
And in one quick movement
   Took from her shoulder
      To be able to have a better look.
This little nun
   Did not know
      What his true intention could be,
But only thought
   That he flirted with her
      And returned quite annoyed.
Now when Tianlu
   Had scrutinized
      This handkerchief for a while,
His whole belly felt
   As if smothered by knives—
      Tears gushed forth like a spring!
"I remember how I
   Now quite long ago
      Gave this to Huixiang as a token;
We brother and sister
   Have now been apart
      For more than five full years.
This handkerchief
   Here in my hands
      Is the same, without any fail,
So this little nun
   Cannot but be
      My own sister."
The more he thought
   The more His Lordship
      Wept in an uncontrollable way:
There in the sutra-hall
   This state-protecting loyal officer
      Was weeping out of control!

In the sutra-hall Wang Tianlu
Was overcome by his anxiety.
Now let's narrate how this little nun

Arrived in the dhyana hall
Where she told her mother,
"That mighty gentleman
Truly lacks all sincerity!
He tried to flirt with me,
This is really way too annoying!"

[Hail to] The Buddhas of the ten directions

"The man took away my handkerchief,
That really fills my innards with rage.
This one my elder brother gave to me!"
At this memory her tears came down.

XXVI. Huixiang Tells Her Mother in Detail about the Handkerchief

[Lanhua Ganzhou]
I think back to that fork in the road at Shuangyang:
Brother and sister, we had left home—how unbearable!
When my brother left me, his tears resembled a spring,
While I wept till my liver and innards were broken.
When he handed me a handkerchief it was this one.
We have been separated now for how many years?
All day long I wept till my eyes had dried out.
Suddenly thinking back
My tears stream down.
If we could meet again, I would thank Heaven,
Thank Heaven!

Tell that when Zhang Suzhen and her daughter had given in to their vexations for quite a while, the nun in charge of affairs urgently asked abbess Suzhen to come to the main hall to write out and recite Wang Tianlu's request. On hearing this, Suzhen hastily dressed properly and came to the main hall. The son did not recognize his mother, and the mother did not recognize her son. When Suzhen had left the house, she still had her hair, and because of the physical work in the house she was somewhat leaner. When she entrusted herself to the Buddha, she had shaved off her hair to leave the household. Now she was wearing a nun's cap and was dressed in a dyed gown. Even though only somewhat older, she did not resemble her earlier self with her filled-out face and large head, so Wang Tianlu could not recognize her. But when he saw that this nun lacked her left eye, he immediately thought of the mother who bore him. "At that time my father had ripped out my mother's left eye and she abandoned the house. She has now been away for these many years and we never had any information. When I think of her, my heart is overcome by grief!" After His Lordship had heaved heavy sighs overcome by vexation for quite a while, he asked the abbess, "Where are you from? At what age did you leave the household? And lose your left eye? Tell me from the beginning."

> When Suzhen heard the questions of His Lordship,
> She knelt down on both knees on the dusty floor.

When Zhang Suzhen
   Heard these questions,
      Tears gushed from her brimming eyes,
"Your Excellency,
   Please kindly listen
      To my clear account of my background,
If you ask
   For my hometown,
      I too am from a distinguished lineage,
Our house was
   Outside Bianliang,
      Straight to the north in Guandong.
Wang Zhongqing
   Of Bali Hamlet
      Was my husband, my man and master,
And I am
   Zhang Suzhen
      Who loved piety and read the sutras.
I gave birth to
   Wang Tianlu
      And also my daughter Huixiang,
But fearing life and death
   And afraid of Impermanence
      I wanted to practice self-cultivation.
I persuaded
   The rich man my husband
      To marry as concubine woman Li,

Thinking that she
    Instead of me
        Could look after household affairs.
But she actually
    Inveigled my husband
        To administer me several beatings.
Then one day
    He had collected loans
        And was as drunk as drunk can be,
And she inveigled
    The rich man my husband
        To rip out one of my eyes,
And I was afraid
    That eventually
        I was in danger of losing my life.
That night at midnight
    I abandoned my children,
        The two of them, son and daughter;
Only then did I flee,
    Come to this convent,
        And shave off my hair to be a nun."
When Wang Tianlu
    Heard this story
        His heart felt as if smothered by knives
And he embraced
    The mother who bore him,
        Thousands of arrows piercing his heart.
He called out,
    "Mother who bore me,
        You may not have recognized me,
But I am
    Wang Tianlu,
        That darling boy that you spoiled.
You fled for your life
    Abandoning us,
        Brother and sister, the two of us,
Causing that woman Li
    To abuse us so much
        We barely escaped with our lives.

Having run off,
   We arrived
      At the fork in the road at Shuangyang,
Where brother and sister
   Separated from each other—
      Straight till the day of today.
When a moment ago
   I saw this handkerchief,
      I wept in an uncontrollable manner:
I handed it to
   My dear little sister,
      As a token to recognize her brother."
The mother embraced her son,
   The son embraced his mother,
      Weeping at the top of their voices;
Then also entered
   His sister Huixiang
      Who was born of the same mother.
Huixiang embraced
   Her dear brother;
      Her heart felt as smothered by knives,
And the three of them
   Wept and cried—
      The emotion would break your heart!
"I only thought
   That our family
      Never would be reunited again!
But my dear son,
   How did you gain office?
      Who was the person to thank?"

Tianlu urged his mother
To be less hurt in her heart,
"On leaving my sister I came to Tong Pass
Where at night I lodged in
The temple of King Guan,
In my dream he taught me
The eighteen military arts.
Upon passing the military examinations
I eventually became commander-in-chief."

"For this I'm indebted first of all to Li Yong
Who led me in killing the Golden Troops.
After exterminating these rebel bandits,
He gave me his daughter as wife."

XXVII. Wang Tianlu and His Mother Are Reunited and Burn Incense to Express Their Thanks to Heaven and Earth

[Zaoluopao]

First they bowed before the holy images of the many Buddhas,
Next they bowed before the dragons, devas, and other divinities.
Those who do good deeds will have a pleasant existence,
Those who commit evil eventually meet with misfortune.
The halls of heaven or the earth-prisons:
Disaster and blessing are not of one kind.
Injustice engenders injustice again:
Don't pride yourself on your strength!
For good or bad, it all depends on the human heart,
On the human heart!

Tell that Wang Tianlu and his mother were reunited. When they had bowed in thanks before Heaven and Earth and the Buddha, Tianlu said, "First of all we will save and deliver the orphan souls, and secondly we will offer assistance to poor people." The news was spread that His Excellency the Commander-in-Chief would donate food and feed the monks as well as save and succor the poor. When Wang Zhongqing and woman Li heard the rumor that the Guanyin Convent would feed the monks and make donations to the poor, the two of them, husband and wife, also arrived at the crimson steps.

When they saw that those many poor had already taken their seats, Zhongqing said, "Let's sit down at the eastern side." The people distributing the rice said, "We start from the western side." When the distribution arrived at the two of them, all soup and rice and finger foods were gone. But Zhongqing said, "We will have something to eat at noon. At noontime we will sit down at the western side." But the people distributing the food started from the eastern side, and when they arrived in front of the two of them, everything was gone. Zhongqing said, "We'll have to wait for this evening to have something to eat. This evening we will sit down in the middle." But the people distributing the rice started from both sides, and it turned out that not even one piece of finger food was left. All other poor people got up and left, but Zhongqing and his wife, tears streaming from their eyes, thought to themselves, "If we were to leave, it is not only quite a distance to the village, but we also are starving. In this desperate situation we can only sing "Lotus Flowers Fall" to beg some food from this Lordship. Let's hope for the best."

    Husband and wife performed "Lotus Flowers Fall,"
    And involuntarily tears coursed down in profusion.

In his anxiety Zhongqing cried out to Blue Heaven,
"What crime have we committed in which existence?
We came but we did not get one bowl of rice to eat,
We stamp our feet, beat our breast, shedding tears."
    At the crimson steps they shouted, cried, and wept,
So disturbing the commander over in the sutra chapel.
"Who are these people clamoring there and shouting?"
He ordered people to go and find out without delay.
    His Lordship addressed them in the following way:
"What caused you trouble? Tell the full reasons!"
Husband and wife knelt down on the dusty floor—
"All your tribulations! But first name your home!"
    "Our house was to the northeast of Bianliang city,
In Bali Hamlet, that is our place of registration.
I am no one else but rich man Wang Zhongqing;
My former wife was sutra-reading Zhang Suzhen.
    Together we had one son, named Wang Tianlu,
And one daughter Huixiang—that's your name.[30]
Later I married woman Li to manage the house,
That was the most inhumane action of my life.
    When drunk I not only beat up woman Zhang,
But I also ripped out an eye—unbearable pain!
She abandoned the family, not leaving a trace,
She abandoned too that couple of little children.
    They demanded from me their dear own mother,
And when I saw them weeping, my heart broke.
I escaped, going to Hangzhou to engage in trade,
While woman Li cruelly maltreated the children.
    The two children fled to no one knows where,
And the ship with my goods sank in the waves.

---

30. As the father recalls the names of his children, he imagines them.

I barely escaped from death, with only my life,
Begging from door to door I made it back home.
   One flash of lightning burned the house to ashes,
Not a single beam or piece of tile was preserved.
The two of us, husband and wife, only could
Try to survive by asking and begging for food.
   The memory of those two, that boy and girl,
Fills me all day with anxiety, breaks my heart;
The mention of my sutra-reading wife Suzhen
Fills my heart with remorse, a killing emotion."
   As Tianlu heard this story, he heaved a sigh:
He was not only angered, but also pained—
The grudge he carried only targeted aunt Li,
He could not carry a grudge against his father.
   So he shouted, "Father, lift your head and look,
Who is this here, wearing this cap and this belt?
Back then you trusted the words of woman Li,
You gave no donations, stopped feeding monks,
   So we, mother and children, left your house—
You amassed greater wealth than Shi Chong.[31]
How have you now arrived here as beggars?
How can one beat Heaven's harsh Principle?"

On hearing this Zhongqing was
Bereft of courage, fear-stricken,
And he loudly called out, "My dear son,
It was I who was in the wrong,
Don't let it rouse you to anger."
At his side this aroused the rage
Of woman Zhang, that Suzhen,
"It is absolutely unallowable
To show mercy to this kind of people!"

> Suzhen shouted to Zhongqing,
> "You need not grieve at all!
> What is the kinship of my
> Son and daughter with you?"

---

31. Shi Chong 石崇 (249–300) used his official career to amass wealth that even the imperial family could not match. He soon became the victim of jealousy and was murdered.

XXVIII. Even Though Tianlu Is Angered, a Younger Generation Cannot Judge an Elder Generation, but Suzhen Makes Things Clear

[Zhuyunfei]
The rich man was heart-broken
And this angered the oh so pious Zhang Suzhen,
"I think of you, lacking all feeling,
Closing down my gate for the wise.
O Heaven,
You listened to woman Li's words
As she inveigled you
To administer me a beating.
What can you say in defense?
All the wealth you amassed—where is it now,
Where is it now?"

Tell that Zhang Suzhen said to Zhongqing, "Each day again you said that by feeding the monks and making donations I was wasting away your money and goods. But how much have you now piled up? Get it out and show it to me!" Wang Zhongqing replied, "Don't lower yourself to my level! At present I have nothing left to say. Would I be willing to go from door to door asking for tea and begging for food if I had any cash?"

Suzhen then ordered her son Wang Tianlu, "Order some military prison wardens to go and throw that woman Li down in front of me so I can take revenge today for her former insults." Hearing this, Wang Tianlu immediately ordered some military prison wardens to bring woman Li before them. Wang Tianlu then said, "What feud did there exist between us and you? But you tried by all means to do in the two of us, brother and sister." Woman Li replied, "Little boy, don't be angered, please forgive me!" But Tianlu ordered his underlings, "Have people strip that rotten slut of her clothes, tie her up tightly, choose a big cudgel, and beat that slave till you have beaten her to death!"

On hearing this, woman Li lost all color
And repeatedly cried out "My husband!"

"My dear husband,
 Please try to reason
  With that darling son of yours,

Let him take pity,
  Show some mercy
    And spare my rotten lousy life!
The two of us
  May have had hard times
    But also had days that were good,
So if I am beaten
  You could not feel
    Comfortable watching the scene."
Now the rich man,
  Not knowing his fault,
    Stepped forward to make a plea,
Shouting, "My son,
  Please consider
    The little love you have for me!
If you beat her,
  Where does that leave
    Me as the father who sired you?
Please consider
  My meager fate
    And spare her rotten lousy life."
When Wang Tianlu
  Heard these words,
    He exploded in thundering rage,
"You are the most
  Shameless person—
    What kind of love can you claim?
Back then you
  Believed all her
    Sweet words and cunning talk,
You and she
  Were the household:
    No affection of father and son!
In all kinds of way
  You beat up my mother
    And even ripped out her eye;
Cruelly you forced her
  And pressured us,
    Separating mother and children.

Just to mention this
   Angers me so
      That I gnash my teeth to shreds
When without shame
   You even urge me
      To feel some pity for her.
How can you
   Claim to be
      The father who sired me?
When I remember
   Your earlier deeds,
      I'd like to pulverize your corpse!
My intention was
   To give her some strokes
      And then allow her to leave,
But she had you
   By your words
      Enlarge the rage in my heart!"
Now woman Li's
   Feet were shackled
      And finger presses were applied;
Once this was done
   It took five hundred times
      Before the pain made her faint.
When he had allowed
   To loosen her fingers,
      The shin presses were applied;
She was also given
   Fifty cudgel strokes—
      Her body was covered in blood.
This woman Li
   Screamed until
      Her mouth was dry, her tongue tired:
She murdered others,
   But failed in her schemes,
      Managing only to murder herself!

Standing to the side Zhongqing
Choked his rage, held his tongue.
Even though the rich man was heart-broken,

He did not have the guts to try
And talk his boy around again,
Because one misspoken word
Had so greatly angered his son.
As his son represented the court,
He was right now the person in power.

[Hail to] The Buddhas of the Ten Directions

> After beating to death that devious woman
> He gave the order to his underling that he
> Would go home and sacrifice at the graves,
> Inviting for those rituals numerous monks.

XXIX. At This Point Wang Tianlu Beats to Death Woman Li in One Go and Invites Monks to Offer Sacrifices to His Ancestors

[Jinzijing]

As a human being to find your spot is hardest of all,
So do not consider time to be an issue of no concern.
Once your hair turns white,
No amount of yellow gold can bring back your youth.
Don't miss the opportunity,
Don't miss the opportunity
And board the Dharma boat right now!

[Jinzijing]

I urge all men and women not to commit violence;
Each should keep to his lot and so conform to fate.
Plant the good roots,
And never harbor jealous thoughts.
Retribution follows,
Retribution follows,
Never off to left or right by an infinitesimal fraction!

Tell that Wang Tianlu had beaten woman Li to death and thrown into a mountain gully for burial.

Now tell that as the whole family was reunited, infantry and cavalry set out on the way to their home to sacrifice at the graves and bow before the ancestors. Twenty-four monks were invited. Within three days they had arrived in Bali Hamlet. The officials and people of the locality had been ordered to erect a large shed to conduct the ceremony for expressing gratitude to Heaven and Earth, the Buddha, as well as dragons and devas, in celebration of their reunion. Right at noontime this moved the bodhisattva Guanyin of the Southern Sea to turn herself into a monk and join the vegetarian feast, reciting,

> Don't laugh at me because I am a fool
> Who all his life is too lazy to meditate.
> As I've suddenly left behind suffering,
> My pleasures are beyond the common.
> My life lasts as long as heaven and earth;
> In pure quietude I never roll up a curtain.
> Living beings, if you can come across me,
> Escape all suffering by boarding the Dharma Boat!

When Suzhen out of the blue heard this monk recite this gātha, she achieved total enlightenment, and she hastily invited the monk and arranged a Purity Hall altar. When the old monk saw that in the middle Śākyamuni was venerated with on his sides Mañjuśrī and Samatabhadra, he smiled mockingly and again recited a gātha:

> Paintings on paper or woodblock prints, don't take them for true:
> They transmit and preserve shadow images to convert the deluded.[32]
> Becoming a Buddha depends on the space of one square inch:
> The thousands of dharmas turn to emptiness all inside your heart.[33]

When Suzhen heard this, she fell to the ground to show her respect and recited the Gātha for Returning Home. This gātha reads,

> That the thousands of dharmas[34] turn to emptiness I too understand;
> I've realized the emptiness of the red dust and of heaven and earth.
> Lucky to encounter the true and wonderful Law of the
> compassionate deity
> I am able in this existence to enter the Pool of the Precious Lotus.

The monk then said, "If you want to return home, you should follow me and recite the name of the Buddha three times."

---

32. Some of the new religions of the Ming rejected the use of images in worship.
33. The heart, said to be one inch square, is believed to be the seat of the inborn Buddha nature.
34. The word "Dharma" (capitalized) refers to the Law or teachings of the Buddha, but "dharma" is used to designate the elements that in their temporary and endlessly changing combinations make up all phenomena of the physical world.

The whole family, now fully enlightened, returned to the Right Way,
As Amitābha received them, helping them board the Dharma Boat.

At the first recitation
   Amitābha arose
      And cleared away all evil karma;
At the second recitation
   They expressed thanks for
      The four graces and the three lives.[35]
At the third recitation
   Auspicious clouds
      Manifested themselves in the sky,
And below the feet
   Of these five people
      Also arose these auspicious clouds.
All of a sudden
   A fragrant breeze wafted
      As they rose up into the sky
And the bodhisattva
   Halfway heaven
      Manifested her golden body.
Wang Tianlu,
   A left golden boy,
      Had descended to the mortal world,
And Huixiang,
   A right jade maiden,
      Had fallen down into the red dust.
Zhang Suzhen
   Was a manifestation
      Of the bodhisattva Vajrāgarbha
And young miss Li
   Was a fan-bearing
      "Hairpins and skirt" atop Taishan.[36]
Wang Zhongqing,
   A curtain-raising general,
      For drunkenness had been banished to earth,

---

35. The four graces refer to the favors bestowed on one by one's parents, all living beings, one's king, and one's teacher. The three lives refer to one's past, present, and future life.

36. Taishan (in Shandong Province) is the holy mountain of the east and the home of the goddess Bixia yuanjun 碧霞元君, who enjoyed widespread veneration in late imperial China. Young miss Li is described as one of her servants.

And woman Li
   Was a Star of Destruction
      Who caused chaos, killing people.
This cause-and-fruit
   Urges all of you
      To turn your head and choose piety:
Even if one lives
   For a hundred years,
      In the end life only is like a dream.
Even if your whole body
   As well as legs and arms are fine,
      Don't pride yourself on being a hero,
Because in case
   King Yama calls,
      There will be no way you can flee.
Your sons and grandsons
   On growing up each have
      The fortune of sons and grandsons:
Pile up yellow gold
   Beyond the Dipper,
      But without blessing it will not stay.
Good sons and grandsons
   Who amount to something
      Can maintain the family fortune,
But those who don't
   Will sell everything off,
      Annihilating all your effort.
This bodhisattva
   Led these five people
      Back to the world of emptiness:
The Buddha's Dharma exhausted,
   The cause and fruit fulfilled,
      And this precious scroll complete.

This scroll has been read completely,
And we convert the merit to the gods.
May each of you make full use of their intelligence!
The Buddha's Dharma is extensive,
The bodhisattva shows compassion.
Let us wish our Imperial King

A sage life of millions of years.
The dharma realm is responsive,
So may we all ascend to the Heaven of Ultimate Bliss.

Hail to the Bodhisattva Guanshiyin Who Ferried across Rich Man Wang's Complete Family so They Might Rise to Heaven

Convert the merit of this performance to the *Single Vehicle School, Limitless Meaning, True Vacuity Miraculous Sutra on Deliverance from Suffering by the Tathāgata*

Convert the merit of this performance to the unsurpassable Buddhas and bodhisattvas.

Prostrate I wish that the sound of the sutra may have loudly and clearly penetrated to the heavenly halls up above, and pierced the dark and dank offices in the earth down below. May those who recite the name of the Buddha depart from the Three Paths and the Prisons below the Earth; may those who commit evil for kalpas on end fall away from the spiritual light, and may those who have obtained enlightenment be led on their way by the Buddhas, emitting a clear light that shines on all ten directions. May in east and west the returning light shine backwards, and in south and north each personally arrive at his home. Board the floating boat of the Unborn to reach the shore, and the little infants will be reunited with their own mother. Once inside the mother's womb you don't have to fear the three disasters, you will join the Dragon-Flower for the eighty-first kalpa, and for all eternity enjoy peace and prosperity. [At the hour of noon the five deities returned to Heaven.

> All evil karma we have created in times long ago
> Originated without reason from cupidity and rage.
> It was generated by our language and our thoughts—
> Banished from Spirit Peak, our true nature is lost.
>   From the Unbeginning down to the present day—
> I now feel remorse for and repent for all my deeds.
> One spark of divine light permeates all creatures,
> Each present kind of rebirth has its personal reason.
>   A womb bears camels, mules, elephants, and horses;
> Eggs generate geese and chickens, make flying birds.
> Moisture generates fishes, turtles, shrimps, and crabs;
> Transformation creates butterflies and dragonflies.

First of all, let us repay Heaven and Earth's favor of covering and carrying;
Secondly let us repay the sun and moon's favor of shining their light on us;
Thirdly let us repay the Imperial King's favor of giving us water and earth;
Fourthly let us repay our father's and mother's favor of feeding and raising us.
Fifthly let us repay the ancestral teacher for transmitting the Dharma in person,
Sixthly let us repay the Gate of Emptiness for kindly transmitting the Dharma.][37]

---

37. The final section starting from "At the hour of noon . . ." is missing in the Ming dynasty manuscript and has been added by the editor Shang Lixin on the basis of a manuscript in the collection of Shanxi University.

Appendix

Early Materials on the Legend of Woman Huang

After Three Lives of Self-Cultivation Woman Wang Ascends to Heaven in Broad Daylight From *Jingangjing zhengguo* (1592)[1]

In the Han dynasty a Mr. Wang from Apricot-Flower Village in Yunhe district of Caozhou was wealthy but had no son. He and his wife sincerely turned toward piety: they respectfully bowed before Buddhas and devas, built bridges, repaired roads, hosted monks, and prayed to dragons and devas to gift them with children. When they had practiced good deeds for ten years and still had no son, they came to resent Heaven and Earth for their stupidity. Husband and wife one night dreamed that the local god of the earth said to them, "You were destined in this life to be rich but childless. Because the two of you have greatly amassed hidden merit and moved the Jade Emperor, he will gift you with half a son. At present there is a priest at the Sizhou Monastery who has promised to read the Diamond Sutra for thirty-six cang[2] but who will be reborn before he has finished the number. That

---

1. This translation is based on the edition of this text in Shang Lixin and Che Xilun, 2015, 279–80.
2. The character *cang* 藏 has several meanings, but here most likely it refers to the total number of the titles included in the Chinese Tripitaka, viz., roughly 5,000 (the exact number differs according the edition). The Nirvana Sutra may be a very short text, but even so 36×5,000 is a very high number.

man should have been pious, but because he was lascivious and covetous he will become a woman on his rebirth. Indra ordered me to report this to you. Afterward you should not resent Heaven and Earth anymore." When husband and wife woke up, their dreams had been identical. When the two of them went to the Sizhou Monastery to make inquiries, there was indeed this monk who had not yet finished reading the Diamond Sutra for thirty-six cang—he was still six cang short. Husband and wife hired twenty-four monks to help him finish quickly. On the day the number had been completed, that monk passed away that very night, seated in meditation, and Wang's wife gave birth to a girl.

When she was six years, her mother passed away. When she was seven, the girl read the Diamond Sutra in order to ferry across her mother, and beginning from this day she afterward read the sutra without interruption. Her father married a woman Hou as her stepmother, and she brought along a son of her own, Hou Qi, who was given to boozing and betting. Her stepmother conspired with him and secretly stole goods of the Wang family, which she gave to Hou Qi for his boozing, betting, and whoring. Mr. Wang realized that this son was no good, and when he left his house one day to collect loans, he entrusted the keys to all the gold and silver and heavy goods in his house to his daughter for safekeeping, and then left to collect these accounts. Her stepmother woman Hou wanted gold and silver to give to her son, and secretly pressured the girl for the keys. Furious because she refused to give them, woman Hou tortured and beat her in all possible ways, stripped her of her clothes, and had her become a barefooted slave in the kitchen. The girl could not stand the suffering and secretly wandered around the grave of her late mother, wishing to commit suicide. When she collapsed from weeping, the god of the mountain and the god of the soil covered her without waking her up. The god of the mountain appeared to Mr. Wang in a dream, informing him that his daughter had been beaten and degraded by woman Hou and was about to die: "You have to hurry back to save her!" When Mr. Wang woke up, it had been a dream, but he hurried back home. Passing by his late wife's grave he met his daughter, who while weeping told him what had happened, and it was exactly identical to his dream. He took the girl along with him, and back at home he punished woman Hou severely.

When Hou Qi saw how his mother was punished, he was filled with hatred. That night he approached the bed, intending to kill his father, rob his possessions, and make the girl his wife. But Heaven would not tolerate this, and he ended up killing his mother. But Hou Qi lodged an accusation that Mr. Wang and his daughter had killed his mother. The first official was an ignoramus and condemned the girl to death by strangulation. Seven days after her death by strangulation, the local god of the soil informed the celestial authorities, who dispatched the Metal Star Great White[3] with a pill of gold and cinnabar to revive her. This is the miracle of her rebirth. When she returned to her home, Hou Qi again lodged his accusation, but this later official was perspicacious and condemned Hou Qi to death by slow slicing[4] for killing his mother. Mr. Wang and his daughter were released and returned to their home.

Once back home, day in and day out, the girl read the sutra. Mr. Wang blamed his daughter for spending too much time each day on reading the sutra and neglecting household affairs, and married her off to butcher Zhao. When she saw that he killed pigs and sheep, woman Wang day and night wept and wailed, urging her husband not to slaughter and kill because the punishments of the earth-prisons would be unsupportable! After ten years she had given birth to two girls and one boy, and her husband too had been converted by her—he stopped killing and read the sutras. Husband and wife practiced self-cultivation together and within three years they emitted a white beaming light like flashes of lightning, and the halls and thrones of the Jade Emperor and the Yama Kings all started to float so they could not hold court. Thereupon they asked the investigating gods, "Who in the world of light has such supernatural powers? Quickly invite them for a meeting." The gods replied, "This is woman Wang." Lads were promptly ordered to invite her.

When woman Wang saw that the lads had come to invite her, she immediately brushed her sleeves, took her leave of her husband and relatives, and passed away. Upon arrival at Ghost Gate Pass, her recitation of the sutra saved millions of sinners on both banks of the Alas River and on the roads of the Yellow Springs. When she arrived in the realm of shade, the Yama Kings all came out and invited her to ascend the hall. Once they were seated as hosts and guest, they invited her to answer their questions about the Diamond Sutra. The effects of her recitation of the sutra were such that a white beaming light shone so brightly in hell as if it was broad daylight. The locked gates of the Fengdu hells opened automatically without any keys; the shackled sinners were all freed of their shackles without any pardon and arrived in front of the hall to thank woman Wang for the power of her sutra. When the sutra was finished, the kings ordered her soul escorted back to earth, but it had already been the third Seventh.[5] Her husband Zhao refused to open the coffin,

---

3. The Metal Star Great White is the planet Venus. This divinity often appears on earth in the guise of a friendly old man on behalf of the Jade Emperor to come to the aid of people in need.

4. This mode of execution is also known as death by a thousand cuts. The main aim was not so much the infliction of pain as the utter destruction of the body.

5. Following death, the soul of the deceased has to appear before the ten judges of the underworld. The soul appears before the first judge on the seventh day following death, before the second

convinced that there was no way that someone who had died during the hottest days of summer could revive after three times seven days, so woman Wang returned to the underworld.

The Yama Kings ordered her escorted to the Zhang family of Caozhou to be reborn as a boy. On the left side of her chest were written the following two lines: "This is the sutra-reading woman Wang / Who returned to earth in the shape of a man," in order to display the eminence of the world of darkness and to urge people on earth to practice goodness. They also determined that he would pass the metropolitan examinations with the rank of Top-of-the-List at the age of eighteen. When he had been appointed as prefect of Caozhou, he passed by the grave of woman Wang and said, "This is the grave of my former life." On the day of his arrival at the prefecture, he promptly summoned butcher Zhao and his children and Mr. Wang to his office and told them everything that had happened. When they refused to believe him, the prefect took off his clothes and said, "These characters on the left side of my chest prove it." The whole population of the prefecture bowed down and praised him, saying, "A living Buddha of great virtue displays his divinity like this!"

The Top-of-the-List said, "In my earlier existences I suffered like this, and the present life was not easily acquired." Immediately he wrote a request,[6] wrapped his seal, and left his post. When Emperor Ling (r. 168–188) heard about this miracle, he by decree awarded him the title "Goodness-Practicing Top-of-the-List." Returning immediately to Caozhou, [the former prefect] devoted himself to self-cultivation together with his former husband, two daughters, and one son, and they all recited the Diamond Sutra for nine years. Then one day five-colored auspicious clouds descended from heaven, and the whole family, all five of them, rose into the sky, emitting a white beaming light. Half a year later the Top-of-the-List returned and also ferried across his father and mother, who likewise ascended to heaven in broad daylight.

---

judge on the fourteenth day following death, before the third judge on the twenty-first day following death, and so forth, until it appears before the seventh judge on the forty-ninth day following death. These days are known as the Seven Sevenths. The soul of the deceased appears before the eighth judge on the one-hundredth day following death, before the ninth judge a full year after death, and before the tenth judge twenty-seven months after death. On each of these dates the relatives of the deceased can contribute to a smooth completion of the procedures by inviting monks and having them recite appropriate sutras (Teiser 1994).

6. A request to be relieved of his official duties.

The *Precious Scroll of Woman Huang* as Partially Included in *The Plum in the Golden Vase*[7]

The answering body[8] permanently saves from suffering, and its origin is neither leaving nor coming. The great Vow of the Buddha Amitābha is great and deep; through his forty-eight vows to ferry across the living beings, he causes each and every person to become aware of their original nature. Amitābha is only the purity of your heart, in charge of ferrying you across the sea of suffering. The huge waves of the sea of suffering prove the wonderful fruit of Bodhi. Those who uphold and recite his name will see their sins annihilated even though as numerous as the sands in the river; those who praise and bless him will see their blessings increased without number, and those who write, copy, read out, and recite [the sutras] will be born in the Lotus Store Heaven. Those who see and hear, receive, and uphold [his name] upon death at the end of their life definitely will go to the Pure Land of the Western Region. All those who recite the name of the Buddha are sure to obtain merits beyond number.[9]

For the sake of mercy, for the sake of mercy, for the sake of great mercy I
   entrust my fate to each and all of the Buddha, Dharma, and Sangha of the
   ten directions
May the Dharma Wheel, constantly turning, ferry across all living beings

   The gāthā reads:

     The unsurpassable and unfathomable subtle and wonderful Dharma
     Is rarely encountered in a hundred thousands of millions of kalpas.
       Now I today have seen it and heard it and can receive and uphold it,
     I desire to understand the Tathāgata's true and substantial meaning.

     As soon as the Precious Scroll of Woman Huang is opened,
     All Buddhas and bodhisattvas descend to attend the recital.
     Incense smoke completely fills the realm of emptiness;
     Voices reciting the Buddha's name shake the whole cosmos.

In the old days when the Han king ruled the world, when the state was prosperous and people lived at peace, a pious-hearted lady was moved to appear in

---

    7. This translation is based on the edition in Shang Lixin, *Baojuan congchao* (2018, 19–26).

    8. The Nirmanakaya, the shape in which the Buddha appears and in any form, for instance as Śākyamuni.

    9. The role of Amitābha was strongly emphasized in some versions of the Unborn Old Mother mythology. See Shek, 1999, 370–72.

this world. Her family lived in Nanhua district of Caozhou, and she was the only daughter of rich man Huang. Well-formed and beautiful, she stuck to a vegetarian diet from the age of seven. She recited the Diamond Sutra each day without fail to repay her parents for their great favors. She even moved the bodhisattva Guanyin to manifest herself in midair. When her parents saw that she recited the sutra all day and did not heed their advice, they one day sought a go-between and on a lucky day and good hour married her off to a son-in-law, who was named Zhao Lingfang and was a butcher by trade.

When the couple had been married for twelve years, they had one son and two daughters.

One day, woman Huang told her husband, "We have been a couple for twelve years and have a lovely son and lovely daughters, but desire, love, and attachments make one sink for all eternity into immersion. I have here a little song, which I would like you to listen to and take to heart." The song reads:

> Husband and wife through a karmic bond we became a couple.
> Even though we have a son and daughters,
> Who is able to withstand Impermanence?
> I humbly hope that you, my lord and master,
> Make up your mind and with me together
> Practice self-cultivation.
> At the end of our lives
> All riches and wealth
> Will rashly be wasted.
> Don't desire fame and profit
> But live your days accepting fate.

Mr. Zhao read the song but was not capable of following her advice. Then one day he took his leave and set out on a trip to Shandong to buy pigs. When woman Huang saw that her husband had left, she slept and rested in a cleaned room, bathed her body, lit incense, and reverentially recited the Diamond Sutra.

> Lingfang at that time had departed for Shandong
> And her three children stayed in the central hall.

> In the western room
> This woman Huang
>   Bathed herself in fragrant water;
> She changed her dress,
> Took off her jewelry,
>   And applied only light makeup.

Toward the West
>   She each day
>   Lit incense, bowing reverentially,
And with serious mien,
>   Collecting precious scrolls,
>   Upheld and recited the Diamond Sutra.
Before she had read
>   The sutra to the end,
>   A fragrant mist spread all around
And the clear voice
>   Of her Buddha-recitation
>   Permeated the highest heavens.
The earth-prisons
>   And heavenly halls
>   Manifested a beaming light,
And as soon as
>   King Yama saw this,
>   Joy showed on his dragon face.
This must be
>   That in the world above
>   A Buddha has been born?
He promptly summoned
>   Two associate judges
>   To search and find all details.
These ghostly judges
>   Reported, "Your Majesty,
>   Please listen and consider:
In Nanhua district
>   Of Caozhou prefecture
>   There lives the pious and good
Sutra-reading
>   Woman Huang
>   Who keeps to a vegetarian diet;
Her pious heart
>   And great merits
>   Amaze and move the heavens!"

Reciting the Diamond Sutra[10]

. . .

---

10. I take this four-syllable line to be the opening line of a hymn the remainder of which was not copied.

On hearing these words King Yama, feeling a great urgency, hastily ordered the two ghosts of Impermanence to go together in greatest haste to Zhao Family Village.

While woman Huang was reading the sutra, she suddenly saw two immortal lads appear before her.

Recite:

>Good persons are invited by these lads,
>But evil people are arrested by yakshas.

Woman Huang, reading the sutra, hastily asked them,
"What kind of lads are you that you come to this place?"
The immortal lads answered her in the following way,
"Pious lady, there is no reason for any anxiety at all.
We are not any family members of the mortal world,
We are virginal lads from the world of shade below.
Because you are presently reading this sutra scroll,
King Yama invites you, pious lady, to his kingdom."
When woman Huang heard this, she was very upset,
And carefully asked these Impermanences in detail,[11]
"Arrest someone with the same name and surname,
But why arrest me to appear before your King Yama!
I would be happy to die hundreds, thousands of times,
But how can I leave my dear baby, my two daughters?
The oldest girl Jiaogu has only recently turned nine,
And how can Banjiao, now six, abandon her mother?
My darling son Changshou is only three years of age,
I always carry him in my arms, how can I forget him?
If the two of you release this one soul and let me live,
I will have many masses conducted for your benefit."
But the immortal lads answered the lady as follows,
"But who can like you recite the Diamond Sutra?"

Woman Huang piteously implored the two lads of good and evil, repeatedly refusing to go to the underworld because she was attached to her children and found it

---

11. The two Impermanences (*wuchang* 無常) are the underworld runners who arrest the souls of those destined to die. One of them is tall, the other short; one of them is dressed in white, the other in black.

EARLY MATERIALS ON THE LEGEND OF WOMAN HUANG

impossible to abandon them and leave them behind. But the immortal lads urged her on. "Pious lady, when the world of shade fetches you in the third watch, you are definitely not allowed an extension till the fourth watch. It's unlike the world of light, where you can adjust a fixed term. The world of shade fetches you, and if we are late, we will be punished, and there will be less room for haggling."

> Woman Huang at this moment made up her mind
> And ordered a female servant to heat up the bath.
> Once she had bathed herself in fragrant hot water,
> She took herself into the Buddha chapel and there
> Sat down in lotus position without saying a word,
> So her one divine true nature greeted King Yama.

Sing:

> [Chujiangqiu]
> This human life is no more than a dream,
> Our time here on earth does not last long.
> When nearing our end each of us is only a wind-blown lamp:
> Within a moment we must return and meet with King Yama,
> So quickly ready your luggage!
> When on Hometown Terrace you look at your home,
> Your children are crying and weeping in a disconsolate way.
> Arranging gongs and beating drums they conduct a mass;
> Wearing hemp, dressed in mourning they order the grave.

Plain prose:[12]

> Do not talk anymore about the distress of Zhao Lingfang—
> Talk about woman Huang on her way to the underworld.
> Very soon she had arrived at the bank of the River Alas,
> Where a golden bridge continued the road she traveled.
> "May I ask what the purpose of this bridge here may be?"
> "It is for people who read sutras, recite Buddha's name!"
> On both sides the Alas was a stream of bloody waves,
> And in that river drifted innumerable souls of sinners.
> Their sad voices, weeping and crying, created a ruckus;

---

12. The Chinese text reads *bai*. I take this to be short for *baiwen* (plain prose), the "stage direction" that introduces passages in prose in the *Hongluo baojuan*. The prose passage, however, has not been copied. This happens a number of times in the following text.

On all four sides black snakes bit their exposed sinews.
Going forward they next arrived at Mt. Wasted Money,
And woman Huang stepped forward, asking the reason.
"When you people in the world of light transform paper,
You throw it away even when it is not yet fully burned.
Because of this the many remaining shreds are swept up;
Collected and piled up, it is called Mt. Wasted Money."
They also passed by the walled City of Unjust Deaths,
Its many orphaned souls there had not yet been reborn.
On hearing this, woman Huang was filled with mercy
And therefore loudly started to recite the Diamond Sutra.
The sinners down in the river all again opened their eyes;
The tortured on Corpse Mountain erected lunar woods.[13]
Lotus flowers opened in seething cauldrons and fiery pools;
Auspicious clouds encased the world without hindrance.
The immortal lads that moment became extremely urgent
And hastily reported this phenomenon to King Yama.

Sing:

[Shanpoyang]

When woman Huang had arrived at the Precious Dark-Welkin Hall,
One little lad went ahead and reported,
"The invited sutra-reading person is here to see you."
When King Yama thereupon had her summoned,
Woman Huang knelt down before the golden steps,
And involuntarily knelt down before His Majesty.
King Yama asked,
"Since which year do you recite the Diamond Sutra?
In which year and month, on which day did Guanyin appear?"
Woman Huang folded her hands, came forward, and replied,
"Since the age of seven I kept to the fast,
And revered the divinities.
Your Majesty, please listen to me,
Ever since I married my husband,
I didn't slacken in reading sutras."[14]

---

13. I do not understand this line. Roy (2010) translates it as "Lunar woods became perceptible to the burned and flayed" (IV, 447).

14. Shang Lixin (2018, 23) treats this song as prose "because it does not too much resemble a lyric." But I follow Roy (2010) in treating it as a song, as the text, prosaic as it may be, clearly rhymes.

Plain prose:

> Lord Yama thereupon hastily transmitted his order,
> "Pious lady, now please listen to these questions.
> How many characters make up the Diamond Sutra,
> How many dots and strokes connect Yin and Yang?
> Which character comes first, and which at the end?
> And which two characters stand right in the middle?"
> Woman Huang, standing below the steps, replied,
> "Your Majesty, let me expound the Diamond Sutra.
> There are five thousand and forty-nine characters,
> Made up of eighty-four thousand dots and strokes.
> The character *ru* comes first, *xing* at the ending,
> And the characters *he* and *dan* stand at the middle."
> Even before she had finished explaining the sutra,
> A beaming light appeared in front of King Yama.
> He raised hands, his dragon face beaming with joy,
> "We allow your soul to return and see the world!"
> When woman Huang heard this, she replied at once,
> "Your Majesty, be so kind as to lend me your ear.
> First of all, I don't want to go to a butcher's house,
> Secondly, I don't want to live in a dyer's home.
> I only want to become the son of a pious family,
> To read the sutras and recite the Buddha's name."
> King Yama took his brush and promptly judged,
> "You'll be a boy in the Zhang family of Caozhou.
> That family has amassed a huge family fortune
> But lacks a filial son to pray at the family graves.
> The rich man and his wife both are pious people
> And their names are renowned through the world."
> She took a bowl of the soul-misleading soup,
> And then rich man Zhang's wife was pregnant.
> After full nine months she gave birth to a boy:
> Two lines written in red appeared on its chest:
> "This boy is the sutra-reading woman Huang,
> Once the wife of Zhao Lingfang of Guanshui.
> Because of the many fruits of sutra-reading
> She could become a man who will live long."
> When rich man Zhang had seen this in person,
> He loved the baby like a pearl, joyfully smiling.

Sing:

[Zaoluopao]
Woman Huang was reborn in the Zhang family:
She had become a man,
The constitution without defect.
When the rich man saw him, he was overjoyed.
After three years, he had grown into a big boy,
And when he was barely seven,
He was intelligent and handsome,
Went to school, learned to write,
And received the name of Junda.
At the age of eighteen he passed the exams with the highest grade.

Now tell that Zhang Junda at the age of eighteen passed the examinations and was appointed as district magistrate of Nanhua district in Caozhou prefecture. Suddenly he remembered that this was his original home. After he had arrived in the district and taken up office, he first handled the king's grain and the state taxes, and afterward organized his office. He dispatched two runners to go and invite Zhao Lingfang: "I have something to discuss with him." The two runners did not dare tarry, and promptly arrived at the house of the Zhao family to invite Lingfang.

Plain prose:

Zhao Lingfang
   Was at his house
      Reading the sutras, reciting the Buddha,
When two runners
   Hastily greeted him.
      Having heard the reason of their visit,
He immediately
   Hastily got dressed
      And arrived inside the district office.
In the court room
   He made his bow
      And narrated his family background.
Magistrate Zhang
   Raised him up
      And ordered him to take a seat;

Discussing the weather
>They sat as guest and host
>>While tea was brought out and served.

"You are my
>Own husband:
>>You're Lingfang, surnamed Zhao,

And I am
>Your late wife,
>>No one else but that woman Huang!

If it strains belief,
>I will in a quiet spot
>>Take off my clothes so you can see

On my left-side chest,
>Written in crimson,
>>The characters that tell my origin.

Our eldest daughter,
>Little Jiaogu,
>>Has already been married off;

Our second daughter,
>Her sister Banjiao,
>>Is married to one Cao Zhen.

Little Changshou
>I dearly remember
>>For keeping guard at my grave."

The two of them
>Mounted their horses
>>And went together to her grave.

The district magistrate, Lingfang, and their son and daughters, five people in total, arrived at the grave of woman Huang. When they opened the coffin, they saw that her features had not changed at all. On their return they conducted rituals for seven days.

When Lingfang was reading the Diamond Sutra, an auspicious snow fluttered down, whereupon the five of them, men and women, together mounted the propitious clouds and rose to heaven. A lyric to the tune of "Immortal by the River" may serve as proof:

> Woman Huang read the sutra and achieved the right fruit:
> On the same day they ascended to Ultimate Bliss.
> The five of them all ascended to Heaven's realm.
> This pious person transmitted Guanyin,
> But that bodhisattva has not yet saved me.

The precious scroll is finished
As the Buddha already knows,
The dharma realm is responsive
So may we all be reborn at the grand gathering.

Hail to the *Single Vehicle School, Limitless Meaning, True Vacuity Miraculous Sutra on Deliverance from Suffering by the Tathāgata*

> May the Buddhas at their ocean-like gathering all hear us from afar
> And let us, as many as the sand of the river, share in the Pure Land.

Prostrate I wish that the sound of the sutra may have loudly and clearly penetrated to the heavenly halls up above, and pierced the dark and dank offices in the earth down below. May those who recite the name of the Buddha depart from the Three Paths and the Prisons below the Earth; may those who commit evil for kalpas on end fall away from the spiritual light, and may those who have obtained enlightenment be led on their way by the Buddhas, emitting a clear light that shines on all ten directions. May in east and west the returning light shine backwards, and in south and north each personally arrive at his home. Board the floating boat of the Unborn to reach the shore, and the little infants will be reunited with their own mother. Once inside the mother's womb you don't have to fear the three disasters, you will join the Dragon Flower for the eighty-first kalpa, and for all eternity enjoy peace and prosperity.

> All multiple evil karma of the sins we committed,
> Lasts from the Unbeginning down to the present.
> Banished from Spirit Peak, your true nature is lost
> But one spark of spiritual light links all beings.

> First of all, let's repay Heaven and Earth's favor of covering and carrying;
> Secondly, let's repay the sun and moon's favor of shining their light on us;
> Thirdly, let's repay the Imperial King's favor of giving us water and earth;
> Fourthly, let's repay our father and mother's favor of feeding and raising us.

Fifthly, let's repay the ancestral teacher for transmitting the Dharma in person,
Sixthly, let repay the Gate of Emptiness[15] for kindly transmitting the Dharma.

Mahā-prajñāparamitā!

---

15. The teachings of the Buddha.

Bibliography

Alexander, Katherine. 2017. "Conservative Confucian Values and the Promotion of Oral Performance Literature in Late Qing Jiangnan: Yu Zhi's Influence on Two Appropriations of the *Liu Xiang baojuan*." *Chinoperl: Journal of Chinese Oral and Performing Literature* 36.2: 89–115.

Anonymous. 1999. "Jingqiao de Yuandai xilou" 精巧的元代戏楼 [A fine stage from the Yuan dynasty]. *Shanxi wenshi ziliao* 1999: 67–69.

Bender, Mark. 2001. "A Description of Telling Scriptures Performances." *Asian Folklore Studies* 60: 101–33.

Berezkin, Rostislav. 2011a. "An Analysis of 'Telling Scriptures' (*Jiangjing*) during the Temple Festivals in Gangkou (Zhangjiagang), with Special Attention to the Status of the Performers." *Chinoperl Papers* 30: 43–94.

———. 2011b. "Scripture-Telling (Jiangjing) in the Zhangjiagang Area and the History of Chinese Storytelling." *Asia Major*, 3rd ser., 24.1: 1–42.

———. 2013a. "The Connection between the Cults of Local Deities and *Baojuan* Texts in Changshu County of Jiangsu: With *Baojuan* Performed in the Gangkou Area of Zhangjiagang as Example." *Monumenta Serica* 61: 73–111.

———. 2013b. "On the Survival of the Traditional Ritualized Performance Art in Modern China: A Case of Telling Scriptures by Yu Dingjun of Shanghu Town Area of Changshu City in Jiangsu Province." *Minsu quyi* 181: 167–222.

———. 2013c. "A Rare Early Manuscript of the Mulian Story in the *Baojuan* (Precious Scroll) Genre Preserved in Russia, and Its Place in the History of the Genre." *Chinoperl: Journal of Chinese Oral and Performing Literature* 32.2: 109–31.

———. 2015. "On the Performance and the Ritual Aspects of the *Xiangshan Baojuan*: A Case Study of Religious Assemblies in the Changshu Area." *Hanxue yanjiu* 33.3: 307–44.

———. 2017. *Many Faces of Mulian: The Precious Scrolls of Late Imperial China*. Seattle: University of Washington Press.

Berezkin, Rostislav, and Vincent Goossaert. 2012–2013. "The Three Mao Lords in Modern Jiangnan: Cult and Pilgrimage between Daoism and *Baojuan* Recitation." *Bulletin de l'École Française d'Extrême Orient* 99: 295–326.

Berezkin, Rostislav, and Boris L. Riftin. 2013. "The Earliest Known Edition of *The Precious Scroll of Incense Mountain* and the Connections between Precious Scrolls and Buddhist Preaching." *T'oung Pao* 99: 445–99.

Bryson, Megan. 2015. "Religious Women and Modern Men: Intersections of Gender and Ethnicity in the Tale of Woman Huang." *Signs: Journal of Culture and Society* 40.3: 623–46.

BIBLIOGRAPHY

Carlitz, Katherine. 1986. *The Rhetoric of "Chin p'ing mei."* Bloomington: Indiana University Press.

Cedzich, Ursula-Angelika. 1995. "The Cult of the Wu-t'ung/Wu-hsien in History and Fiction: The Religious Roots of the *Journey to the South*." In *Ritual and Scripture in Chinese Popular Religion: Five Studies*, edited by David Johnson, 137–218. Berkeley: Chinese Popular Culture Project.

Che Xilun 车锡伦. 1990. "*Jin Ping Mei cihua* zhongde xuanjuan—jianlun *Jin Ping Mei cihua* de chengshu" 金瓶梅词话中的宣卷— 兼论金瓶梅词话的成书 [Performance of precious scrolls in *Plum in the Golden Vase*—also discussing the date of composition of the *Tale with Songs on Plum in the Golden Vase*]. *Ming Qing xiaoshuo yanjiu* 1990: 360–74.

Che Xilun 車錫倫. 1997. *Zhongguo baojuan yanjiu lunji* 中國寶卷研究論集 [A collection of articles on China's precious scrolls]. Taipei: Xuehai chubanshe.

———, comp. 1998. *Zhongguo baojuan congmu* 中國寶卷總錄 [A comprehensive catalogue of China's precious scrolls]. Taipei: Zhongguo wenzhesuo choubeichu.

———. 2002. *Xinyang, jiaohua, yule—Zhongguo baojuan yanjiu ji qita* 信仰, 教化, 娛樂: 中國寶卷研究及其他 [Belief, education, and entertainment: Studies on China's precious scrolls and other subjects]. Taipei: Xuesheng shuju.

Che Xilun 车锡伦. 2007. "Foshuo Wang Zhongqing dashisan Shoujin baojuan *manlu* 佛说王忠庆大失散手巾宝卷漫录" [Some comments on *The Precious Scroll, as Preached by the Buddha, of the Handkerchief: How Wang Zhongqing Lost Everything*]. *Shaoguan xieyuan xuebao* 28.4: 9–13.

———. 2009. *Zhongguo baojuan yanjiu* 中国宝卷研究 [Studies on China's precious scrolls]. Guilin: Guangxi shifan daxue chubanshe.

Cole, Alan. 1998. *Mothers and Sons in Chinese Buddhism*. Stanford: Stanford University Press.

Dong Zaiqin 董再琴 and Li Yu 李豫. 2008. "*Jin Ping Mei cihua* zhong nigu xuanjuan huodong benshi laiyuandi kaosuo" 金瓶梅词话中尼姑宣卷活动本事来源的考索 [An inquiry into the activities of nuns preaching precious scrolls in the *Tale with Songs on the Plum in the Golden Vase* and the origin of their contents]. *Beijing huagong daxue xuebao* 64.4: 45–50.

Dudbridge, Glen. 1978. *The Legend of Miao-shan*. London: Ithaca Press.

———. 2004. *The Legend of Miaoshan*. Rev. ed. Oxford: Oxford University Press.

Feng Ye 封野. 2019. *Nanjing fosi xulu* 南京佛寺叙录 [A list of Buddhist establishments in Nanjing]. Nanjing: Fenghuang chubanshe.

Fong, Grace S. 2004. "Female Hands: Embroidery as a Knowledge Field in Women's Everyday Life in Late Imperial and Early Republican China." *Late Imperial China* 25.1: 1–58.

Fou Si-houa. 1951. "Catalogue des Pao-kiuan 寶卷總錄" [A catalogue of precious scrolls], in Centre d'études sinologiques de Pékin, *Melanges sinologiques* 1951: 41–103.

Fu Xihua 傅惜華. See Fou Si-houa

Glahn, Richard von. 1991. "The Enchantment of Wealth: The God Wutong in the Social History of Jiangnan." *Harvard Journal of Asiatic Studies* 51: 651–714.

Goodrich, Ann Swann. 1964. *The Peking Temple of the Eastern Peak: The Tung-yüeh Miao in Peking and Its Lore with Twenty Plates. Appendix: Description of the Tung-yüeh Miao of Peking in 1927 by Janet R. Ten Broeck*. Nagoya: Monumenta Serica.

Grant, Beata. 1989. "The Spiritual Saga of Woman Huang: From Pollution to Purification." In *Ritual Opera, Operatic Ritual: "Mu-lien Rescues His Mother" in Chinese Popular Culture*, edited by David Johnson, 224–304. Berkeley: Chinese Popular Culture Project.

———. 1995. "Patterns of Female Religious Experience in Qing Dynasty Popular Literature." *Journal of Chinese Religions* 23: 29–58.

Grant, Beata, and Wilt L. Idema. 2011. *Escape from Blood Pond Hell: The Tales of Mulian and Woman Huang*. Seattle: University of Washington Press.

Guo Lamei 郭腊梅. 2018. *Suzhou xiqu bowuguan cang baojuan tiyao* 苏州戏曲博物馆藏宝卷提要 [Summaries of precious scrolls in the collection of the Suzhou Museum of Opera and Theater]. Beijing: Guojia tushuguan chubanshe.

Guo, Qitao. 2003. *Exorcism and Money: The Symbolic World of the Five-Fury Spirits in Late Imperial China*. Berkeley: Center for Chinese Studies.

Haar, Barend J. ter. 2017. *Guan Yu: The Religious Afterlife of a Failed Hero*. Oxford: Oxford University Press.

Ho, Chiew Hui. 2019. *Diamond Sutra Narratives: Textual Production and Lay Religiosity in Medieval China*. Leiden: Brill.

Hou Ching-lang. 1975. *Monnaies d'offrande et la notion de tresorie dans la religion chinoise*. Paris: Collège de France Institut de Hautes Études Chinoises.

Huang Jing 黄靖. 2013. *Baojuan minsu* 宝卷民俗 [Precious scrolls and popular customs]. Suzhou: Guwuxuan chubanshe.

Huijiao 慧皎. 1992. *Gaoseng zhuan* 高僧傳 [Biographies of eminent monks], annotated by Tang Yongtong 湯用彤 and edited by Tang Yixuan 湯依玄. Beijing: Zhonghua shuju.

Huitu sanjiao yuanliu soushen daquan (wai erzhong) 绘图三教源流搜神大全外二中 [The illustrated great survey in search of the gods: the origins and developments of the three teachings, with two more versions]. 1990. Shanghai: Shanghai guji chubanshe.

Idema, Wilt L. 2008. *Personal Salvation and Filial Piety: Two Precious Scroll Narratives of Guanyin and Her Acolytes*. Honolulu: University of Hawai'i.

———. 2009. *Heroines of Jiangyong: Chinese Narrative Ballads in Women's Script*. Seattle: University of Washington Press.

———. 2015. *The Immortal Maiden Equal to Heaven and Other Precious Scrolls from Western Gansu*. Amherst, NY: Cambria Press.

Ji Qiuyue 纪秋悦. 2019. "Lun *Hongluo baojuan* de wenben yu xinyang zhi bian" 论红罗宝卷的文本与信仰之变 [On the changes in the text and the beliefs of the *Precious Scroll of Red Gauze*]. Master's thesis, Fudan University.

Ji Shijia 季士家. 1981. "Nanjing Zhonghuamen jianzhu shulüe" 南京中华门建筑书略 [A short description of the construction of the Zhonghuamen Gate in Nanjing]. *Wenwu ziliao congkan* 5: 154–57. Beijing: Wenwu chubanshe.

Johnson, David. 1995. "*Mu-lien* in Pao-chüan: The Performance Context and Religious Meaning of the *Yu-ming Pao-ch'uan*." In *Ritual and Scripture in Chinese Popular Religion: Five Studies*, edited by David Johnson, 55–103. Berkeley: Chinese Popular Culture Project.

Lévy, André. 1971. "Le motif d'Amphitryon en Chine: 'Les cinq rats jouent de mauvais tours à la capitale orientale'" [The motif of Amphitryon in China:

"The five rats create havoc in the eastern capital"], in *Études sur le conte et le roman chinois*, 115–46. Paris: École française d'Extrême Orient.
Li Fang 李昉, comp. 1960. *Taiping guangji* 太平廣記 [Comprehensive records of the Great Peace reign-period]. Beijing: Zhonghua shuju.
Li Shiyu 李世瑜. 1961. *Baojuan zonglu* 寶卷總錄 [General catalogue of precious scrolls]. Beijing: Zhonghua shuju.
———. 2007. *Baojuan lunji* 寶卷論集 [Collected articles on precious scrolls]. Taipei: Lantai chubanshe.
Li Yu 李豫 a.o. 2010. *Shanxi Jiexiu baojuan shuochang wenxue diaocha baogao* 山西介休宝卷说唱文学调查报告 [A report on the research on the prosimetric literature of precious scrolls in Jiexiu, Shanxi]. Beijing: Shehui kexue wenxian chubanshe.
Li Yuhang. 2012. "Embroidering Guanyin: Construction of the Divine through Hair." *East Asian Science, Technology and Medicine* 36: 131–66.
Liu Huiru 刘祎如. 2018. "Xiqu, xiaoshuo he shisu baojuan dui lianhualao de wenhua xuanze ji wenxue shuxie" 戏曲小说和世俗宝卷对莲花落的文化选择及文学书写 [The cultural selection and literary description of "beggars' songs" in plays, novels, and popular precious scrolls]. *Qiqiha'er daxue xuebao* 2018.10: 107–10, 120.
Liu Lili 刘丽丽. 2012. "Lüelun Nüzhen wenzi" 略论女真文字 [A short discussion of the Jürched script]. *Shiji qiao* 190 (2012, 12): 35–36.
Lu Yupeng 陆羽鹏, ed. 1989. *Chengdeshi gushi juan di'erjuan* 承德市故事卷第二卷 [The second volume of stories from Chengde city]. Beijing: Zhongguo minjian wenyi chubanshe.
Ma Xisha 马西沙. 1986. "Zuizao yibu baojuan de yanjiu" 最早一部宝卷的研究 [A study of the earliest precious scroll]. *Shijie zongjiao yanjiu* 23: 56–72.
Ma Xisha 馬西沙, ed. 2012. *Zhonghua zhenben baojuan* 中華珍本寶卷 [China's rare precious scrolls]. Beijing: Shehui kexue wenxian chubanshe.
Mair, Victor H. 1983. *Tun-huang Popular Narratives*. Cambridge: Cambridge University Press.
———. 1988. *Painting and Performance: Chinese Picture Recitation and Its Indian Genesis*. Honolulu: University of Hawai'i Press.
———. 1989. *T'ang Transformation Texts: A Study of the Buddhist Contribution to the Rise of Vernacular Fiction and Drama in China*. Cambridge, MA: Harvard University Press.
Meng Dan 孟丹 and Wang Guangxian 王光先, eds. 2011. *Zhongguo minjian gushi quanshu Henanxian juan Wushe minjian gushi quanji 2* 中国民间故事全书河南县卷武陟民间故事全集 2 [The complete collection of Chinese folktales: Henan districts. The complete collection of folktales from Wushe 2]. Zhengzhou: Zhongzhou guji chubanshe.
Mu Soeng. 2000. *The Diamond Sutra: Transforming the Way We Perceive the World*. Boston: Wisdom Publications.
Overmyer, Daniel L. 1976. *Folk Buddhist Religion: Dissenting Sects in Late Traditional China*. Cambridge, MA: Harvard University Press.
———. 1991. "Women in Chinese Religions: Submission, Struggle, Transcendence." In *From Beijing to Benares: Essays on Buddhism and Chinese Religion in Honour of Prof. Jan Yün-hua*, edited by Koichi Shinohara and Gregory Schopen, 91–120. Oakville, ON: Mosaic Press.

———. 1999. *Precious Volumes: An Introduction to Chinese Sectarian Scriptures from the Sixteenth and Seventeenth Centuries.* Cambridge, MA: Harvard University Asia Center.

Roy, David Tod, trans. 2010. *The Plum in the Golden Vase, or, Chin P'ing Mei.* Vol. 4, *The Climax*. Princeton, NJ: Princeton University Press.

Sawada Mizuho 澤田瑞穂. 1975. *Sōbo Hōkan no kenkyū* 増補寶卷の研究 [A study of precious scrolls, expanded edition]. Tokyo: Kokusho kankokai.

Scott, Janet Lee. 2007. *For Gods, Ghosts, and Ancestors: The Chinese Tradition of Paper Offerings*. Seattle: University of Washington Press.

Seiwert, Hubert, in collaboration with Ma Xisha. 2003. *Popular Religious Movements and Heterodox Sects in Chinese History*. Leiden: Brill.

Shang Lixin 尚丽新. 2018. *Baojuan congchao* 宝卷丛抄 [Selections from precious scrolls]. Taiyuan: Sanjin chubanshe.

Shang Lixin 尚丽新 and Che Xilun 车锡伦. 2015. *Beifang minjian baojuan yanjiu* 北方民间宝卷研究 [A study of popular precious scrolls from the north]. Beijing: Commercial Press.

Shek, Richard. 1999. "Challenge to Orthodoxy: Beliefs and Values of the Eternal Mother Sects in Sixteenth- and Seventeenth-Century China." *Early Modern History* 3.3: 355–93.

Shi Nai'an 施耐菴 and Luo Guanzhong 羅貫中. 2009. *Shuihu quanzhuan jiaozhu* 水滸全傳校注 [A critical and annotated edition of the *Complete Tale of the Water Margins*], annotated by Wang Liqi 王利器. Vol. 2. Shijiazhuang: Hebei jiaoyu chubanshe.

Sun, Xiaosu. 2019. "Praying at the Xiangshan Altar of Wishes: Performance of the *Precious Scroll of Incense Mountain* in the Greater Suzhou Area." *CHIME* 21: 159–68.

Teiser, Stephen F. 1988. *The Ghost Festival in Medieval China*. Princeton, NJ: Princeton University Press.

———. 1994. *The Scripture of the Ten Kings and the Making of Purgatory in Medieval Chinese Buddhism*. Honolulu: University of Hawai'i Press.

Waley, Arthur. 1960. *Ballads and Stories from Tun-huang*. London: Allen and Unwin.

Wang Jianchuan 王見川. 1999. "Tang Song guanyu xinyang chutan—jiantan qiyu fojiao zhi yinyuan" 唐宋官與信仰初探— 兼談其與佛教之因緣 [A preliminary discussion of the belief in Guan Yu during the Tang and the Song, with comments on its link to Buddhism]. *Yuanguang foxue xuebao* 6: 111–24.

Wang Shucun 王樹村, Li Fuqing 李福清 (Boris L. Riftin), and Liu Yushan 刘玉山, eds. 1989. *Sulian cang Zhongguo minjian nianhua zhenpin ji* 苏联藏中国民间年画珍品集 [A collection of fine examples of Chinese popular New Year prints preserved in the Soviet Union]. Beijing: Zhongguo renmin meishu chubanshe.

Wood, Frances, and Mark Barnard. 2010. *The Diamond Sutra: The Story of the World's Earliest Dated Printed Book*. London: British Library.

Wu Qingzhou 吴庆州. 2005. "Ming Nanjing chengchi de junshi fangyu tixi yanjiu" 明南京城池的军事防御体系研究 [A study of the military defense system of walls and moats of Nanjing during the Ming]. *Jianzhushi* 2005.2: 86–91.

Wu Ruiqing 吴瑞卿. 2018. *Fu Xihua cang baojuan shouchaoben yanjiu* 傅惜华藏宝卷手抄本研究 [A study of the manuscript copies of precious scrolls in the collection of Fu Xihua]. Beijing: Xueyuan chubanshe.

Xu Yunzhen 许允贞. 2016. "'Liu Xiangnü' gushi nüxing yishi yanjiu: Yi chuanqi *Shuangxiu ji*, *Liu Xiang baojuan*, pinghua *Liu Xiang nü* wei zhongxin" 刘香女故事女性意识研究：以传奇双修记, 刘香宝卷, 评话刘香女为中心 [A study of female awareness in the story of Liu Xiangnü, focusing on the *chuanqi* play *A Tale of Paired Self-Cultivation*, the *Precious Scroll on Liu Xiang*, and the *pinghua* narrative *Liu Xiangnü*], in Wang Dingyong 王定勇, ed., *Zhongguo baojuan guoji yantaohui lunwenji* 中国宝卷国际研讨会论文集 [Collected articles of the International Conference on China's Precious Scrolls], 198–208. Yangzhou: Guangling shushe.

Xue Runmei 薛润梅. 2018. "Lun *Jin Ping Mei* zhongde xuanjuan shuxie" 论金瓶梅中的宣卷书写 [On the description of precious scroll performances in *Plum in the Golden Vase*]. *Taiyuan shifan xueyuan xuebao* 17.4: 17–22.

Yang Taikang 楊太康 and Cao Zhanmei 曹占梅, comps. 2006. *San Jin xiqu wenwu kao* 三晉戲曲文物考 [A study of the drama-related cultural relics of Shanxi]. Taipei: Shi He Zheng jijinhui.

Yang Zihua 杨子华. 2006. "*Jin Ping Mei* suo miaoxie de Fojiao wenyi: xuanjuan" 金瓶梅所描写的佛教文艺：宣卷 [Buddhist literary arts as described in the *Plum in the Golden Vase*: The performance of precious scrolls]. *Yunyang shifan gaodeng zhuanke xuexiao xuebao* 26.2: 34–39.

Yü, Chün-fang. 2001. *Kuan-yin: The Chinese Transformation of Avalokiteśvara*. New York: Columbia University Press.

Zhang Tianyou 张天佑 and Zhang Xipin 张曦萍. 2019. "Lun Hexi baojuan zhongde cixiu yishu" 论河西宝卷中的刺绣艺术 [On the art of embroidery in the precious scrolls from Western Gansu]. *Lanzhou wenli xueyuan xuebao* 35.6: 15–20.

Zheng Zhenduo 鄭振鐸. 1959. *Zhongguo suwenxue shi* 中國俗文學史 [A history of Chinese popular literature]. Beijing: Wenxue guji kanxingshe.

Zhou Shaoliang 周紹良. 1990. "Ji Mingdai xinxing zongjiao de jiben baojuan" 記明代新興宗教的幾本寶卷 [Some precious scrolls of the new religions of the Ming]. *Zhongguo wenhua* 1990.3: 23–30.

Zong Li 宗力 and Liu Qun 刘群. 1986. *Zhongguo minjian zhushen* 中国民间诸神 [The popular gods of China]. Shijiazhuang: Hebei renmin chubanshe.

CPSIA information can be obtained
at www.ICGtesting.com
Printed in the USA
LVHW041537260721
693702LV00001B/96